D1341924

H. W. Longfellow.

LONGFELLOW
& HIS POETRY

BY

OLIPHANT SMEATON M.A. F.S.A.
Lecturer on Shakespeare in Heriot-Watt College Edinburgh

LONDON : GEORGE G.
HARRAP & COMPANY
3 PORTSMOUTH STREET
KINGSWAY W.C. MCMXIII

One volume of the Poetry and Life Series
published by AMS Press

Reprinted by special arrangement with
George G. Harrap & Co. Ltd., London

From the edition of 1913, London

First AMS edition published in 1971

Manufactured in the United States of America

International Standard Book Number:
Complete Set: 0-404-52500-8
This Volume: 0-404-52533-4

Library of Congress Catalog Card Number: 76-120966

AMS PRESS INC.
NEW YORK, N.Y.   10003

GENERAL PREFACE

A GLANCE through the pages of this little book will suffice to disclose the general plan of the series of which it forms a part. Only a few words of explanation, therefore, will be necessary.

The point of departure is the undeniable fact that with the vast majority of young students of literature a living interest in the work of any poet can best be aroused, ~nd an intelligent appreciation of it secured, hen it is immediately associated with the character and career of the poet himself. The cases are indeed few an' far between in which much fresh light will r ɔʋ be thrown upon a poem by some knowledge of the personality of the writer, while it will often be found that the most direct—perhaps even the only—way to the heart of its meaning lies through a consideration of the circumstances in which it had its birth. The purely æsthetic critic may possibly object that a poem should be regarded simply as a self-contained and detached piece of art, having no personal affiliations or bearings. Of the validity of this as an abstract principle nothing need now be said. The fact remains that, in the earlier stages of study at any rate, poetry is most valued and loved when it is made to seem most human and vital ; and the human and vital interest of poetry can be most surely brought home to the reader by the biographical method of interpretation.

5

GENERAL PREFACE

This is to some extent recognised by writers of histories and text-books of literature, and by editors of selections from the works of our poets ; for place is always given by them to a certain amount of biographical material. But in the histories and text-books the biography of a given writer stands by itself, and his work has to be sought elsewhere, the student being left to make the connexion for himself ; while even in our current editions of selections there is little systematic attempt to link biography, step by step, with production.

This brings us at once to the chief purpose of the present series. In this, biography and production will be considered together and in intimate association. In other words, an endeavour will be made to interest the reader in the lives and personalities of the poets dealt with, and at the same time to use biography as an introduction and key to their writings.

Each volume will therefore contain the life-story of the poet who forms its subject. In this, attention will be specially directed to his personality as it expressed itself in his poetry, and to the influences and conditions which counted most as formative factors in the growth of his genius. This biographical study will be used as a setting for a selection, as large as space will permit, of his representative poems. Such poems, where possible, will be reproduced in full, and care will be taken to bring out their connexion with his character, his circumstances, and the movement of his mind. Then, in

GENERAL PREFACE

addition, so much more general literary criticism will be incorporated as may seem to be needed to supplement the biographical material, and to exhibit both the essential qualities and the historical importance of his work.

It is believed that the plan thus pursued is substantially in the nature of a new departure, and that the volumes of this series, constituting as they will an introduction to the study of some of our greatest poets, will be found useful to teachers and students of literature, and no less to the general lover of English poetry.

WILLIAM HENRY HUDSON

POEMS QUOTED
IN WHOLE

POEMS QUOTED
IN PART

POEMS QUOTED IN PART

LONGFELLOW AND HIS POETRY

FOR many a year, on this side the Atlantic at least, the name of Henry Wadsworth Longfellow was synonymous with well-nigh all that was known of American poetry. In those days the hemispheres were relatively almost as far apart as the earth and the stars. In the early days of the Victorian era Washington Irving, Emerson, and the subject of our study were the names in Transatlantic letters best known to British readers, with perhaps those of Bryant, Ticknor, and Fenimore Cooper. Nay, as late as 1860, in a work of the standing of Collier's "History of English Literature" (Nelson's School and College Series), Bryant, Longfellow, Lydia Sigourney, and Edgar Allan Poe were ranked as the outstanding singers of the New World, a supplementary list, presumably of those regarded as of minor importance, being added in which the names of Pierpont, Dana, Sprague, Percival, Halleck, and Lowell appeared. To this a note in small type was appended that " John Greenleaf Whittier, a Quaker poet, might be added to this list." That he, to-day esteemed by many, both here and in his own land, as the greatest and most stimulating singer of America, is dismissed with a line reveals the wide difference between the critical standpoint then and now.

Yet why was the song native to the Transatlantic soil so persistently depreciated, not only in Britain but even in America itself ? The causes were precisely those which have, in like manner, operated to delay the rise of a native literature in Canada, Australia, New Zealand, and, in fact, all new colonies. These may briefly be summarized as : (1) The exaggerated respect paid to the productions of the present as well as to those of the past in the literature of the Mother Country ; (2) so complete an absorption in the task of nation-making that the development of the literary and artistic qualities is checked ; (3) the lack of a well-to-do leisured class interested chiefly in literature and art ; (4) the fact that the people have never passed through the stage of national infancy, that era of legend-lore and superstition that plays so large a part in the early history of many races. On the last point Mr. E. C. Stedman says :

Our people are removed from the wondercraft and simple faith prevailing among the common folk of other lands than our own. The beautifying lens of fancy has dropped from our eyes. Where are our forest and river legends, our Lorelei, our Venusberg, our elves and kobolds ? We have old-time customs and traditions, and they are quaint and dear to us, but their atmosphere is not one in which we freely move. . . . More clearly to understand how far and in what way our poets have felt the lack of background of social contrasts and of legendary and specific incident, we may observe the literature of some region where different conditions exist. In an isolated country of established growth and quality a native genius soon discovers his tendency and proper field. Look at Scotland. Her national melodies were ready and waiting for Burns, her legends, history, and traditions for Walter Scott. The popular tongue, costumes, manners, all distinctively and picturesquely her own, affect the entire outcome of her song and art.

So much for difficulties in the way of the rise of a native literature. Glance now at obstacles retarding its development when the start has once been made. Curious it is that when a native American literature had been created by the genius and labour of Bryant, Poe, Haliburton, Washington Irving, Cooper, Longfellow, Emerson, Whittier, Holmes, Hawthorne, Lowell, Whitman, Ticknor, Bancroft, &c., and a recognition, more or less reluctant, of its intrinsic greatness had been wrung from British critics, a tendency manifested itself to claim for Britain a sort of reflected credit in all that the genius of the Transatlantic world had achieved either in prose or verse. British critics affected to be pleased that the writers of the great Republic were descendants of the same stock as themselves, proving themselves, in fact, veritable chips of the same good old Anglo-Saxon block, while native American critics echoed the sentiment, until a fashion crept into criticism of appraising the value of a Transatlantic work accordingly as it manifested or lacked qualities cognate with those prominent in English literature.

In fact, the *rôle* of America as assigned to her by more than one leading British critic was to play the " sedulous ape " of English literary modes ; otherwise to imitate the attitude of the writers of Rome toward Grecian literature, in accordance with which canon a man was esteemed original in precise ratio as he copied his model with slavish fidelity. This was the characteristic of most of those "pre-Longfellow singers " who form the bulk of the Griswold collection, and who reveal among themselves and toward their models, the English didactic poets of the eighteenth century, a similarity in thought and form that ere long becomes intolerably monotonous. In this matter, as Mr. Grant White well says, it is the spirit, not the letter, that giveth life, and we must pay regard rather to the flavour than to the form and colour of the fruit, to the distinctive character, not to the speech and aspect, of the personage. To clinch the point let us recall the following apt words of Mr. E. C. Stedman : " Unless the feeling of our home poet be novel, unless his vision be a fresh and distinctive vision, unless these are radically different from the French or German or even the English feeling and vision—they are not American and our time has not yet come ! "

To Henry Wadsworth Longfellow, therefore, American literature owes the important service of dissociation from a past which was really to it an alien past in all but language, and a linking up to a new cycle of scenery, customs, aspirations, sentiments, and ideals, whereby the merely colonial outlook slowly but surely developed into the broadly national survey.

How was it that Longfellow's genius, when in the fullness of time he came to reveal it, was ambivocal, that is, gave expression on the one side to a culture as catholic as it was consummate—embracing as it did all those European literatures in which were to be found pearls of great price—and on the other to a ready sympathy with the customs, scenes, and sentiments associated with his native land ? The reply is not far to seek. In himself he represented two entirely distinct, yet by no means alien, strains of descent, the Royalist or moderate Puritans, who had a keen appreciation of all culture, and the theocratic or Biblical Puritans of the extreme type, to whom a Royalist was a man of sin and culture a gin of the devil. We must always remember the existence of these two " wings " in the Puritan party—those that were less and those that were more rigid in their adherence to religious doctrine. For example, the Pilgrim Fathers were loyal to the Crown, and had no sympathy with the policy of the Independents who followed them to America some thirty years later, after having achieved the evil notoriety of being responsible for the execution of Charles I. Both of these strains met in Longfellow, and thus is explained the anomaly of the dual interests which possessed him, first toward the broad literary culture of Europe, and secondly toward the life and aspirations of American patriotism. He found qualities germane to his own instincts and genius in the characteristics of both hemispheres, and his mind fed equally upon the intellectual, social, and artistic phenomena of European learning and upon the impressive facts and forces that literally thrust themselves on his attention in connexion with nation-making in the great Republic of the West. Puritanism had its flowers of culture in prose and verse that bloomed as unmistakably upon its gnarled boughs as did the first growth on the carefully trained branches that sprang from the Cavalier stem. It is folly, therefore, to argue that the poetry and romance of the great struggle that went on between King and People on both sides of the Atlantic lay wholly with the supporters of King and Church. ⋅ Cavalier poetry is sensuously beautiful and seductively fascinating, but has it the lofty spiritual afflatus of Milton's inspired lays or Marvell's odes, or, to take examples from America, the sterling force of such pieces as the famous "Ode on the Death of Nathaniel Bacon," or the poems of Uriah Oakes (1631–1681), or Michael Wigglesworth (1631–1705), or Anne Bradstreet (1612–1672), or John Norton (1651–1716)?

New England, of old the centre of a noble type of Puritanism, has always led the culture of the North American States, alike as colonies

and as members of the Union. Its outstanding
and most constant trait in verse has been a
truly 'Wordsworthian sense of fellowship with
the indwelling spirit of natural scenery, with
a keen sense of its magic and mystery and a
ready recognition of its subtle speech. During
the past century this has been more markedly
the case than ever, and no influence has been
more potent in fostering the growth of this
characteristic in New England verse than
Henry Wadsworth Longfellow. To him the
scenery of the country around his native place
was passing dear, and he has made us familiar
with well-nigh every outstanding feature of it
in various poems. Born at Portland, the chief
seaport, though not the capital city, of Maine—
one of the six States that go to form New
England—on February 27, 1807, the son of a
highly respected lawyer named Stephen Longfellow, who had married Zilpah, the eldest
daughter of General Peleg Wadsworth, a
warrior of note during the War of Independence,
Longfellow was thus descended from a Puritan
and a Pilgrim stock on both sides. Further, as
we learn, he was the child of a cultured household, born not only with a poet's voice and ear,
but, as Stedman says, with an aptitude for
letters amounting to a sixth sense, and a bookish-
ness assimilative as that of Charles Lamb or
Leigh Hunt.

Portland, "the Forest City," is beautiful
to-day and will always be beautiful, with its
great gulf of rolling blue, Cape Elizabeth at one

horn, and at the other the miniature archipelago called Casco Bay, the low hills of Munjoy and Bramhall piled up behind the houses, backed again by stretches of the noblest woodland, while every street is lined on either side with graceful shade trees.

· When Longfellow was about five years of age, during the war of 1812 between America and Britain, a naval battle took place off the coast of Maine, when the British brig " Boxer," Captain S. Blythe, was captured by the American brig " Enterprise," Lieutenant W. Burrows. The latter towed its prize into Portland Harbour, and both the commanders, who had been killed in the engagement, were buried side by side at the base of Munjoy Hill.

The scenery of the district surrounding the town, as well as the circumstances of the sea-fight, which must have been witnessed by Longfellow, are thus recorded by him in " My Lost Youth " in terms of graphic narrative and vivid poetic charm :

MY LOST YOUTH

Often I think of the beautiful town
  That is seated by the sea ;
Often in thought go up and down
The pleasant streets of that dear old town,
  And my youth comes back to me.
    And a verse of a Lapland song
    Is haunting my memory still :
  " A boy's will is the wind's will,
And the thoughts of youth are long, long thoughts."

LONGFELLOW & HIS POETRY

I can see the shadowy lines of its trees,
    And catch, in sudden gleams,
The sheen of the far-surrounding seas,
And islands that were the Hesperides
    Of all my boyish dreams.
        And the burden of that old song,
        It murmurs and whispers still :
    " A boy's will is the wind's will,
And the thoughts of youth are long, long thoughts."

I remember the black wharves and the slips,
    And the sea-tides tossing free ;
And Spanish sailors with bearded lips,
And the beauty and mystery of the ships,
    And the magic of the sea.
        And the voice of that wayward song
        Is singing and saying still :
    " A boy's will is the wind's will,
And the thoughts of youth are long, long thoughts."

I remember the bulwarks by the shore,
    And the fort upon the hill ;
The sunrise gun, with its hollow roar,
The drum-beat repeated o'er and o'er,
    And the bugle wild and shrill.
        And the music of that old song
        Throbs in my memory still :
    " A boy's will is the wind's will,
And the thoughts of youth are long, long thoughts."

I remember the sea-fight far away,
    How it thundered o'er the tide !
And the dead captains, as they lay
In their graves o'erlooking the tranquil bay,
    Where they in battle died.

And the sound of that mournful song
   Goes through me with a thrill :
" A boy's will is the wind's will,
And the thoughts of youth are long, long thoughts."

I can see the breezy dome of groves,
   The shadows of Deering's Woods ;
And the friendships old and the early loves
Come back with a sabbath sound, as of doves
   In quiet neighbourhoods.
     And the verse of that sweet old song,
     It flutters and murmurs still :
" A boy's will is the wind's will,
And the thoughts of youth are long, long thoughts."

And Deering's Woods are fresh and fair,
   And with joy that is almost pain
My heart goes back to wander there,
And among the dreams of the days that were,
   I find my lost youth again.
     And the strange and beautiful song,
     The groves are repeating it still :
" A boy's will is the wind's will,
And the thoughts of youth are long, long thoughts."

In " The Prelude " and in " The Ropewalk "
he also recalls those golden days of childhood
and youth which, though they appear to pass
so slowly while we are looking out from among
them toward the years that are to be, seem, when
we gaze regretfully back upon them from the
desert of age with its remorse over lost oppor-
tunities, to have flitted by swift as the flash of
summer's lightning. This phase of thought
appears in the former piece, wherein he says :

LONGFELLOW & HIS POETRY

Pleasant it was, when woods were green,
   And winds were soft and low,
To lie amid some sylvan scene,
Where, the long drooping boughs between,
Shadows dark and sunlight sheen
   Alternate come and go ;

Or, where the denser grove receives
   No sunlight from above,
But the dark foliage interweaves
In one unbroken roof of leaves,
Underneath whose sloping eaves
   The shadows hardly move.

Beneath some patriarchal tree
   I lay upon the ground ;
His hoary arms uplifted he,
And all the broad leaves over me
Clapped their little hands in glee,
   With one continuous sound.

The green trees whispered low and mild ;
   It was a sound of joy !
They were my playmates when a child,
And rocked me in their arms so wild !
Still they looked at me and smiled,
   As if I were a boy ;

And ever whispered, mild and low,
   " Come, be a child once more ! "
And waved their long arms to and fro,
And beckoned solemnly and slow ;
Oh, I could not choose but go
   Into the woodlands hoar ;

Into the blithe and breathing air ;
   Into the solemn wood,

Solemn and silent everywhere !
Nature with folded hands seemed there,
Kneeling at her evening prayer !
  Like one in prayer I stood.

Visions of childhood !   Stay, oh stay !
  Ye were so sweet and wild !
And distant voices seemed to say,
" It cannot be !   They pass away !
Other themes demand thy lay ;
  Thou art no more a child ! "

Other poems could be named in which he makes reference to that joy in life which was his portion in youth, but we have already given more space to this period of his career than our plan warrants.   On the other hand, unless we get the fact impressed on our mind that it was the influence of local surroundings playing on his susceptible nature in early years that made him the strongly objective poet he became, we lose the key that will unlock the secret of his art.

His education at school and college was prosecuted upon a system calculated to secure a liberal culture alike in the arts and sciences. He was an intensely studious lad, disliking sports of all kinds.   Accordingly when in " The Ropewalk " we note him recalling the joys of " kite-flying "—

Then the schoolboy with his kite,
Gleaming in a sky of light,
  And an eager upward look—

we know that he must have experienced the

joy by proxy, inasmuch as history records he never flew a kite in his life.

Formerly the youth of the State of Maine who desired academic training had to betake themselves to Harvard, in Massachusetts. A few years before our poet's birth, however, a small university, Bowdoin College, had been started at Brunswick, in Maine. Thither Longfellow went. His career was most distinguished. He proved himself easily "First Student" of his year, Nathaniel Hawthorne being one of his classmates. At nineteen he graduated, and so highly did the Senatus regard his position that they assigned to him the honour of delivering one of the three "English Orations" on the graduation day. He chose the subject "Our Native Writers," and delivered an address highly appreciated by those who heard it. During his senior examination for degree Longfellow had made a translation of one of Horace's odes. This achievement so delighted one of the college trustees that, to the amazement of every one, he proposed the nineteen-year-old graduate for the new chair of Modern Languages in the university. The appointment was approved by the board, and Longfellow was directed to proceed to Europe and to spend three years in fitting himself for the position.

To give the reader some idea of Longfellow's precocity and extraordinary powers, I propose to quote his "Hymn of the Moravian Nuns," written in his eighteenth year. During his three-years college course he contributed in all seventeen pieces to the literary page of the " Portland Gazette." Of these he accounted five —" An April Day," " Sunrise on the Hills," " Woods in Winter," " Autumn," and the " Hymn of the Moravian Nuns "—as worthy to be retained in the collected edition of his works. A stern critic at all times of his own compositions, he certainly sacrificed some poems that were worthy of preservation. The " Hymn " shows how carefully, even at this stage, he had studied the principles of prosody, metrical arrangement, assonance, and the like. To win the poet's chaplet of bays he unquestionably spared no pains in preparation. The following is the " Hymn " :

HYMN OF THE MORAVIAN NUNS OF BETHLEHEM

AT THE CONSECRATION OF PULASKI'S BANNER

When the dying flame of day
Through the chancel shot its ray,
Far the glimmering tapers shed
Faint light on the cowlèd head ;
And the censer burning swung,
Where, before the altar, hung
The blood-red banner, that with prayer
Had been consecrated there.

And the nuns' sweet hymn was heard the while,
Sung low in the dim, mysterious aisle.

" Take thy banner !   May it wave
Proudly o'er the good and brave ;

When the battle's distant wail
Breaks the sabbath of our vale,
When the clarion's music thrills
To the hearts of these lone hills,
When the spear in conflict shakes,
And the strong lance shivering breaks.

" Take thy banner ! and, beneath
The battle-cloud's encircling wreath,
Guard it !—till our homes are free !
Guard it !—God will prosper thee !
In the dark and trying hour,
In the breaking forth of power,
In the rush of steeds and men,
His right hand will shield thee then.

" Take thy banner ! But, when night
Closes round the ghastly fight,
If the vanquished warrior bow,
Spare him !—By our holy vow,
By our prayers and many tears,
By the mercy that endears,
Spare him !—he our love hath shared !
Spare him !—as thou wouldst be spared !

" Take thy banner !—and if e'er
Thou shouldst press the soldier's bier,
And the muffled drum should beat
To the tread of mournful feet,
Then this crimson flag shall be
Martial cloak and shroud for thee."

The warrior took that banner proud,
And it was his martial cloak and shroud !

" Sunrise on the Hills " betrays a study, careful and profound, of Bryant's nature-poems

and of Bryant's master, William Wordsworth.
The following passage recalls the famous one
in Wordsworth's "Poems of Sentiment and
Reflection" :

> If thou art worn and hard beset
> With sorrows, that thou wouldst forget,
> If thou wouldst read a lesson, that will keep
> Thy heart from fainting and thy soul from
>   sleep,
> Go to the woods and hills !   No tears
> Dim the sweet look that Nature wears.

What is this but a statement in different words
of Wordsworth's noble lines :

> But hark ! how blithe the throstle sings !
>   He, too, is no mean preacher.
> Come forth into the light of things,
>   Let Nature be your teacher.
> She has a world of ready wealth,
>   Our minds and hearts to bless—
> Spontaneous wisdom breathed by health
>   Truth breathed by cheerfulness.
> One impulse from a vernal wood
>   May teach you more of man,
> Of moral evil and of good,
>   Than all the sages can.

II

TO every man the culture he wins in life
is of two kinds—that derived from study
and that from travel. The rule holds
good in both cases, therefore, that the greater
the labour expended, the richer the return.

LONGFELLOW & HIS POETRY

The more books a man thoroughly masters with keen and unwavering attention, the wiser he becomes in the learning and the lore hidden therein. With equal cogency, the conclusion may be drawn on the other side that the more widely a man travels, reaping the while ever richer harvests of the quiet eye of observation, the more will his soul be filled with that wealth of culture which the accumulated literary and historic stores of lands other than his own alone can give.

The youthful professor-elect of Bowdoin, after graduating in the autumn of 1825, spent the winter in hard study among the "dry bones" of the grammars of the principal European languages. He found it, as he said, "maddening drudgery," but he persevered with noble resolution. In May 1826 he left America, and arrived in France during the following June. In Paris he studied French with enthusiasm and resolution until February 1827, receiving great kindness from many distinguished Frenchmen, such as Jules Janin. From Paris he journeyed to Spain, and at Madrid met Washington Irving, then engaged on his " Life of Columbus." Irving took a deep interest in the youthful professor, and was of material help in directing his Spanish studies. From Spain Longfellow bent his steps toward Italy in December, and in Florence and Padua and Rome threw himself with eager zest into mastering the Italian language and literature. There he lingered until the end of July 1828, when he proceeded to Germany. Of that great country, not yet welded into a homogeneous political whole, he studied the speech and literary monuments under a celebrated Berlin professor until July 1829, when, his three years of preparation for which he had stipulated being completed, he turned his face homeward.

Wisely he had confined himself to the four more important European languages, French, German, Italian, Spanish. These he thoroughly mastered. To a remarkable linguistic aptitude he united a rare faculty for detecting analogies in the various allied tongues. In other words, he displayed a ready genius for comparative grammar, which later in life was to arouse the admiration of Professor Whitney.

To the literary monuments, however, rather than to the linguistic niceties of the several allied families of speech he felt drawn, and he speedily familiarized himself with all that was noble in the literatures in question. His whole being was possessed by a surpassing love of letters. To tap the minds of the mighty masters of thought in Europe was to him an enterprise of prime importance, because so much depended on it in connexion with the welfare of the institution wherein his work was to lie. Well does Mr. W. Tirebuck say of him and his work :

England imbibed the Continental influences as a whole mainly through literature : America is now imbibing them mainly through men, through the migrating thousands of Europe. It was for this change of condition, for this new circumstance in the evolution
28

of mankind, that Longfellow wrote. He was the poet for the newly forming nation out of many nations, and, viewed in this light, Longfellow's journeys to Europe to equip himself for the Bowdoin and Harvard professorships by acquiring the European languages were something more than the journeys of a schoolmaster in search of lessons for his pupils. They were rather the journeys of a bardic ambassador going to the fatherland of song to learn how to reach the hearts of the adopted sons of his country.[1]

Longfellow felt to the full the sacred, almost prophetic, character of the vocation of the writer who realizes his responsibilities and accounts literary labour a joy for ever. He was expressing his own sentiments and his own sense of responsibility when in " Hyperion," chap. vii., he makes Paul Flemming, under which personality Longfellow portrayed his own character and idiosyncrasies, thus address his friend the Baron of Hohenfels :

The lives of scholars in their cloistered stillness : literary men of retired habits, and professors who study sixteen hours a day and never see the world but on a Sunday—Nature has no doubt, for some wise purpose, placed in their hearts this love of literary labour and seclusion. Otherwise, who would feed the undying lamp of thought ? But for such men as these a blast of wind through the chinks and crannies of this old world or the flapping of a conqueror's banner would blow it out for ever. The light of the soul is easily extinguished. And whenever I reflect on these things I become aware of the great importance of the individual

[1] Introduction to " Longfellow's Prose " (Scott Library), by William Tirebuck.

fame of scholars and literary men. I fear that it is far greater than the world is willing to acknowledge.

A man who took his work as seriously as this would not certainly be one to scamp or to shirk the duties of the hour, onerous though they might be. Longfellow's three years and a half of study were now over. He had filled the obligation laid upon him by Bowdoin College of preparing himself in every possible way for the chair of Modern Languages. The call of home and of academic duties was now sounding loudly in his ears, and in July 1829 he set sail for America, to be welcomed on landing by many friends. In the following September he commenced work at Bowdoin College. Though he did not teach the elements of the various languages, that being left to assistants, from the professor it was that the students gained their real enthusiasm for literature. He taught them to grasp the principles of comparative literature, otherwise those universal standards of taste and excellence which underlie the great works of genius in all lands.

Of his life at Bowdoin we have few memorials in his works. His academic duties, though not too onerous, were sufficient to keep him busily employed. He found time, however, to contribute pretty regularly to the " North American Review," to translate the " Coplas " of Don Jorge Manrique, an early Spanish poet, and to write a sketch of his travels, "Outre-Mer."

LONGFELLOW & HIS POETRY

The " Coplas " was issued in 1833, while Part I of " Outre-Mer " appeared late in the same year and Part II in 1834. Along with the " Coplas " were published a few translations from the Spanish of Lope de Vega and Francisco de Aldana, others from the Italian of Dante, the French of Charles d'Orléans, and the German of Uhland, Stockmann, Müller, and Salis. Despite the fact that Longfellow was a marvellously accurate renderer of the thoughts of others into English verse, sometimes he was tempted to exercise the right of paraphrasing rather than of translation. Note the following lines in the " Coplas," which are designedly more emphasized than the original quite warrants. They depict the state of mind in which Longfellow at times found himself ere he had a helpmate to share the load of life's cares.

O World ! so few the years we live,
Would that the life which thou dost give
 Were life indeed !
Alas ! thy sorrows fall so fast,
Our happiest hour is when at last
 The soul is freed.

Our days are covered o'er with grief,
And sorrows neither few nor brief
 Veil all in gloom ;
Left desolate of real good,
Within this cheerless solitude
 No pleasures bloom.

Thy pilgrimage begins in tears
And ends in bitter doubts and fears
 Or dark despair ;

31

Midway so many toils appear,
That he who lingers longest here
Knows most of care.

Such sentiments would be unnatural from a
young man of twenty-five, with life's prizes
well within his grasp, were they not merely the
result of that pseudo *tædium vitæ* which it
was fashionable for the student of Goethe's
"Werther" to feel. The wave of "Wertherism,"
although now beginning to subside, had still
a strange fascination for unmarried youths
of a sentimentally imaginative cast of mind.
Thackeray's wicked satire "The Sorrows of
Werther," in which he laughed languishing
Wertherism out of fashion—

Werther had a love for Charlotte
Such as words could never utter.
Would you know how first he met her ?
She was cutting bread-and-butter—

was not due yet for a few years. Longfellow was
to be cured of this phase of feeling, through which
most young men pass, by another means—he
married young, and in domestic bliss found
nepenthe for his pain.

His choice fell upon Miss Mary Storer Potter,
a beautiful girl whom he had known since
she was a little maid in short dresses, as she
was a daughter of his father's near neighbour
in Portland. Though she had no pretensions
either to culture or to intellectual power, her
nature was a subtle blending of sweetness and
of light. Longfellow realized at once that the

half of life's cares vanished when such a beacon
flashed its rays over the maelstrom of existence.
His love for his wife was profound, and she did
much to draw the retiring scholar-poet from the
seclusion in which he fain would have lived.   By
all she was loved and idolized.   There is no
poem in his works to which we could definitely
point and say, " That is Longfellow's tribute to
his first wife." In " Hyperion," however,
written after her death, under the guise of
Paul Flemming we have the poet in fictional
autobiography delineating the desolation of
heart and soul which befell him when
she who had been his other-self passed on
into the Eternal Silence.   He thus writes in
chapter i. :

The setting of a great hope is like the setting of the
sun.   The brightness of our life is gone.   Shadows of
evening fall around us, and the world seems but a dim
reflection, itself a broader shadow.   We look forward
into the coming lonely night.   The soul withdraws into
itself.   Then stars arise and the night is holy.   Paul
Flemming had experienced this, though still young.
The friend of his youth was dead. The bough had broken
" under the burden of the unripe fruit."   And when,
after a season, he looked up again from the blindness
of his sorrow, all things seemed unreal.   Like the man
whose sight had been restored by miracle, he beheld
men as trees walking.   His household gods were
broken.   He had no home.   His sympathies cried
aloud from his desolate soul, and there came no answer
from the busy, turbulent world around him.   He did
not willingly give way to grief.   He struggled to be
cheerful—to be strong.   But he could no longer look

c

into the familiar faces of his friends. He could no longer live alone, where he had lived with her. He went abroad that the sea might be between him and the grave. Alas ! between him and his sorrow there could be no sea but that of time !

(After five years of unremitting industry and eager interest in the work of his chair at Bowdoin College, Longfellow was alike surprised and gratified to receive in December 1834 an offer from the authorities of Harvard College to become the successor of Ticknor as the Smith Professor of Modern Languages in that great university) Attached to the offer was the gratifying addendum that, should he so desire it, the board would grant him a year's leave to spend in Europe ere he assumed the duties. Needless to say, the proposal was gratefully accepted.

In April 1835 Longfellow and his wife set sail for Europe. He was anxious to render himself more intimately acquainted with German litera-ture, also to acquire a fuller knowledge of the Scandinavian cycle of languages. He spent three weeks in London, where he had passed three golden days during his former visit. As Professor Eric S. Robertson says, he went into the best society in London as became a man of some note furnished with good introductions. His days and his nights in the English metro-polis were full of intellectual gaiety :

He breakfasted with Sir John Bowring ; dined with the Lockharts ; at Babbage's met Jane Porter, Lady

Morgan, Abraham Hayward, and the sister beauties, Mrs. Blackwood and Lady Seymour. At Lady Dudley Stuart's he listened to the singing of Rubini and Grisi. One day Carlyle came to talk delightfully to the poet and his wife for half an hour. Carlyle had them home to tea and took them to visit Chantrey's studio. On the whole, the Longfellows were most struck with Mrs. Carlyle, whom they described as " a lovely woman with simple and pleasing manners and as accomplished as modest."

While in London an arrangement was come to with Mr. Bentley whereby an English edition of " Outre-Mer " was issued. On its appearance the " Spectator " declared that it rivalled Washington Irving's " Sketch Book."

London, with its pleasant friendships, was exchanged in June for Stockholm, where Longfellow studied Swedish with Professor Lignell of Upsala ; Finnish he picked up through intercourse with a Lutheran pastor named Mallin, who also was a poet, while in Copenhagen his Danish studies were directed by Mr. Bolling, the chief librarian of the city. In this way six months were passed in assiduous labour, though a dark cloud of anxiety was beginning to show upon the horizon, caused by the uncertain health of his wife.

From the Scandinavian cycle of languages the time came presently to devote attention to the Germanic cycle. He therefore went to Holland to study Dutch at Amsterdam, The Hague, and Delft. His wife's health, however, grew steadily worse, and, to his intense grief, at

Rotterdam on November 29 she died. Only during the last few days of her illness did the fact come to his knowledge that she had been suffering the most acute anguish for weeks, and enduring it with a smiling face that she might not hinder her beloved husband's work. The blow to him was overwhelming, yet of the real deadliness or poignancy of the stroke no one knew, for he was not one to wear his heart upon his sleeve. One circumstance alone was noticeable, a strain of overwhelming sadness passed now into the sweetness of his smile —a sadness that was never wholly to be lost. His wife's memory he enshrined in one of the most exquisite elegies in our literature, "Footsteps of Angels," in which it is manifest how deep was the impression the heroism of the frail girl had made upon him. Nothing in the poet's work more surely touches us than this plaintive cry from his sad heart.

FOOTSTEPS OF ANGELS

When the hours of Day are numbered
    And the voices of the Night
Wake the better soul, that slumbered,
    To a holy, calm delight ;

Ere the evening lamps are lighted,
    And, like phantoms grim and tall,
Shadows from the fitful firelight
    Dance upon the parlour wall ;

Then the forms of the departed
  Enter at the open door ;
The belovèd, the true-hearted,
  Come to visit me once more ;

He, the young and strong, who cherished
  Noble longings for the strife,
By the roadside fell and perished,
  Weary with the march of life !

They, the holy ones and weakly,
  Who the cross of suffering bore,
Folded their pale hands so meekly,
  Spake with us on earth no more !

And with them the Being Beauteous,
  Who unto my youth was given,
More than all things else to love me,
  And is now a saint in heaven.

With a slow and noiseless footstep
  Comes that messenger divine,
Takes the vacant chair beside me,
  Lays her gentle hand in mine.

And she sits and gazes at me
  With those deep and tender eyes,
Like the stars, so still and saint-like,
  Looking downward from the skies.

Uttered not, yet comprehended,
  Is the spirit's voiceless prayer,
Soft rebukes, in blessings ended,
  Breathing from her lips of air.

37

> O, though oft depress'd and lonely,
>   All my fears are laid aside ;
> If I but remember only
>   Such as these have lived and died !

Her example strengthened him also to suffer silently and be strong, while his fears of what the dark and indefinite future might bring all vanished—

> If I but remember only
>   Such as these have lived and died.

In one other poem of this period he referred to the extraordinary power which the moral example of his deceased wife exercised over him. She was not intellectually strong, but as an ethical force for good she was a veritable tower of strength. Therefore he adds in " The Light of Stars " :

> And thou, too, whosoe'er thou art,
>   That readest this brief psalm,
> As one by one thy hopes depart,
>   Be resolute and calm.
>
> O fear not in a world like this,
>   And thou shalt know ere long—
> Know how sublime a thing it is
>   To suffer and be strong.

Crushing though his grief was, Longfellow was not the man to allow it to dominate his nature. He resumed his work in view of the importance of the post for which he was preparing. After completing his studies at Rotterdam, he went on to Heidelberg, and there, amid a group of highly intellectual people, the keen edge of his sorrow was gradually dulled. There he met for the first time his own great countryman, William Cullen Bryant, the poet and author of that sublimest of all musings on death, "Thanatopsis"; also Herr Wuttermaier, a lawyer and leader of the Liberal Party; Schlosser, the professor of modern history, whom De Quincey so unjustly satirized; Gervinus, the Shakespeare scholar; Reichlin-Meldegg, the authority on modern German literature, and several others. Here, too, he laid the foundations of that profound acquaintance with German literature which rendered him beyond question the first authority in America on that subject. From Heidelberg he passed onward to the Tyrol and to Switzerland. At Interlaken he met with the family of Mr. Appleton, a wealthy American, whose daughter, a beautiful girl of twenty, was not only possessed of great and varied culture, but was endowed with intellectual powers of no ordinary range. Though Longfellow's heart was still too full of sorrow to permit of any other image finding a lodgment there than that of her who so recently had passed away to her rest, there can be no doubt that even at this early stage in their intercourse Frances Elizabeth Appleton had done much to soothe the poet's grief into a feeling of tender regret over the demise of one who had been prematurely called upon to pay the inevitable debt of nature.

We find in "Hyperion" a record of the romance of Longfellow's second marriage, until the parting of the lovers. For seven years the poet was a widower, and during that time Miss Appleton's influence over him was always steadily increasing. The portrait of the lady as drawn in " Hyperion " was unmistakable, and at first she was not a little vexed to find herself publicly ticketed as the poet's ideal. He thus described " Mary Ashburton," that being the thin veil of pseudonymity under which he limned the person and character of her who was to be his second wife :

Old Froissart tells us in his Chronicles that when King Edward beheld the Countess of Salisbury at her castle gate he thought he had never seen before so noble nor so fair a lady ; he was stricken thereupon to the heart with a sparkle of pure love that endured long after ; he thought no lady in the world so worthy to be beloved as she. And so likewise thought Paul Flemming when he beheld the English lady in the fair light of a summer morning. I will not disguise the truth. She is my heroine ; and I mean to describe her with great truth and beauty, so that all shall be in love with her, and I most of all.

Mary Ashburton was in her twentieth summer. Like the fair maiden Amoret, she was sitting in the lap of womanhood. They did her wrong who said she was not beautiful, and yet

> ". . . she was not fair,
> Nor beautiful ;—those words express her not.
> But O, her looks had something excellent,
> That wants a name ! "

Her face had a wonderful fascination in it. It was such a calm, quiet face, with the light of the rising soul shining so peacefully through it. At times it wore an expression of seriousness, of sorrow even ; and then seemed to make the very air bright with what the Italian poets so beautifully called the " lampeggiar dell' angelico riso "—the lightning of the angelic smile. And O, those eyes, those deep unutterable eyes, with " down-falling eyelids, full of dreams and slumber," and with them a cold living light, as in mountain lakes at even, or in the river of Paradise, for ever gliding

> " With a brown, brown current,
> Under the shade perpetual that never
> Ray of the sun lets in, nor of the moon."

I dislike an eye that twinkles like a star. Those only are beautiful which, like the planets, have a steady lambent light, are luminous but not sparkling. Such eyes the Greek poets give to the Immortals. The lady's figure was striking. Every step, every attitude was graceful and yet lofty, as if inspired by the soul within. Angels in the old poetic philosophy have such forms ; it was the soul itself imprinted on the air. And what a soul was hers ! A temple dedicated to Heaven, and, like the Pantheon at Rome, lighted only from above. And earthly passions in the form of gods were no longer there, but the sweet and thoughtful faces of Christ and the Virgin Mary and the Saints. Thus there was not one discordant thing in her, but a perfect harmony of figure and face and soul—in a word, of the whole being. And he who had a soul to comprehend hers must of necessity love her, and, having once loved her, could love no other woman for evermore.

" Hyperion " was published in 1839. The last sentence in the above extract was a virtual declaration of his passion by the poet, and there can be little doubt it was understood by Frances Appleton as such. Though her delicacy was offended by the publicity of this " stage wooing," and though for a time thereafter she kept Longfellow at arm's length, the nobility of his nature and the transparent purity and honesty of the man's whole character so grew upon her that slowly but surely her heart was won.

In addition to the poet's own winning personality there was another factor in the problem of how the heart of Frances Appleton was to be gained that went far to break down any scruples or hesitation on the score of delicacy or modesty which the lady may have felt. In December 1836 Longfellow had returned to America and entered upon his academic duties at Harvard. The splendid welcome he received and the crowds of students he attracted were all evidence of the high esteem in which the new professor was held. That, however, was not all. Though " Hyperion," issued in 1839, seriously wounded Miss Appleton's sense of modesty, the reading public as a whole, and the critical reviews almost without exception, praised the unique and outstanding character of the work.

Further, during the same year Longfellow's first acknowledged collection of original poems appeared, entitled " Voices of the Night," and fairly carried the country by storm. Never before in America had there been literary success so brilliant, so unalloyed, so thoroughly well deserved,

42

yet so modestly borne. The volume included
" The Prelude," "Hymn to the Night," "A
Psalm of Life," " The Reaper and the Flowers,"
"The Light of the Stars," "Footsteps of Angels,"
" Flowers," " The Beleaguered City," " Midnight Mass for the Dying Year," also the
translations he had made from various European
languages, which had already appeared in many
of the existing journals and periodicals, and,
finally, the " Early Poems," which dated back
to his student years.

The gem of the collection was, of course, " A
Psalm of Life." It had seen the light anony-
mously in the " Knickerbocker Magazine " in
the autumn of 1838, and had instantly become
popular. Reprinted far and near, men were
eagerly demanding the name of the author,
when the " Voices of the Night " issued from
the press and answered the question. The
success of the volume was phenomenal, that
result being largely due to the rare popularity
of the " Psalm." Speaking as it did to every
heart then suffering from that weary unrest
which afflicted all sorts and conditions of men,
it preached a gospel of Duty, sane, hopeful,
and performable by all, because based on a faith
that scorned the fine-spun dogmas of mere
religiosity, but bowed before the doctrines of a
Christ-given creed.

The four stanzas that have infused heart and
hope into many a despairing voyager over life's
solemn main are those that proclaim that
evangel which is the " God-spell " of the

workers of to-day, viz. the stern reality of life
and its duties, the responsibility attaching to
faithful and unflinching discharge of the day's
task, and finally the certainty that honestly
discharged labour either brings its own material
reward or is its own ethical reward in the
consciousness of doing right :

> Life is real !   Life is earnest !
>   And the grave is not its goal :
> " Dust thou art, to dust returnest,"
>   Was not spoken of the soul.
>
> Not enjoyment, and not sorrow,
>   Is our destined end or way ;
> But to act that each to-morrow
>   Find us farther than to-day.
>
> Trust no Future, howe'er pleasant !
>   Let the dead Past bury its dead !
> Act ! act in the living Present,
>   Heart within and God o'erhead !
>
> Let us, then, be up and doing,
>   With a heart for any fate ;
> Still achieving, still pursuing,
>   Learn to labour and to wait.

Few poems have been more widely quoted and
reprinted than " A Psalm of Life."   Translated
into many languages, it has conveyed the same
calm, clear code of duty to all and sundry : " Do
your duty and leave the issue to God."

Frances Appleton would have been callous
indeed had she remained indifferent to the subtle
pleading of such advocates to her heart. She was

44

woman enough to be impressed by the wave of affection that swept out from the hearts of the American people to this singer who touched their souls to such high and holy issues. When all loved him so profoundly, was she to stand aloof —she the one woman he desired ? She would have been more than human had she not been influenced by all that was happening around her during those seven years that elapsed between the date of their parting at Interlaken in Switzerland in November 1836 and the time in 1843 when she consented to become his wife.

Singularly enough this period was one of the most prolific in the whole course of his literary career, and it is curious that it should synchronize with that epoch when Frances Appleton was slowly but surely becoming the dominating impulse in his life. The difference between the influence exercised by her and that which his first wife, Mary Storer Potter, had possessed over him was just the distinction existing between the power wielded by a gentle, beautiful, clinging soul of strong domestic tendencies and that of a sturdy, self-reliant, keenly intellectual, and highly cultured nature, eager to help by criticism as well as to elevate by inspiration. During the short life of his first wife the poet did next to nothing save along the lines of his academic work. No sooner do we see the image of Frances Appleton rising over the horizon of his existence than we find him striving to realize his own ideals alike in prose and verse. The explanation was that Miss Appleton detected in him from the

first a subtle, almost imperceptible, but yet none
the less persistent strain of dilettantism, which
was leading him to regard literature as a thing
of such high ideals that publication must not be
resorted to until the author is satisfied by the
witness of his own judgment and the criticism
of friends that he can refine the work no
farther. Of many an excellent author such a
course of action has been the ruin. To rely too
much on the opinion of others and too little on
his own had been Longfellow's failing. The
verdict of the "Five of Clubs," an informal
association of his friends, Felton, Sumner,
Hillard, and Cleveland, upon his work did him
more harm than good. All to his advantage was
it, therefore, that a stronger influence than
theirs speedily began to assert itself and to
challenge the correctness of their criticisms by
stimulating him to assert his own good sense.

The marvellous fecundity of the period 1837–43
is a testimony to the increasing sway Frances
Appleton was exercising over Longfellow's life.
He had been devoting attention to what he called
"the National Ballad"—in other words, the
narration in metrical form of striking incidents
in the history of America. Of this he says in his
diary :

I have broken ground in a new field, viz. ballads, beginning with the "Wreck of the Schooner Hesperus "
on the reef of Norman's Woe, in the great storm of a
fortnight ago. I shall send it to some newspaper. I
think I shall write more. The *National Ballad* is a virgin

soil here in New England, and there are great materials. Besides, I have a great notion of working on the *people's* feelings. I am going to have it printed on a sheet with a coarse picture on it. I desire a new sensation and a new set of critics. . . . Felton laughs and says, " I wouldn't."

This was the point on which the influence of Frances Appleton was stronger than that of the " Five of Clubs." She strongly favoured the idea, and though it was not carried out in the suggested form, she advised the poet to write these national ballads, inasmuch as they appealed to the great heart of the people. The inspiration came upon him one evening as he was sitting by the fireside. He went to his desk and did not rise until after a few hours' work he had completed the ballad, which appeared in the " New World " for January 1840. Until encouraged to attempt the ballad form by Miss Appleton, he had distrusted his own powers. The brilliant reception accorded to " The Wreck of the Hesperus " proved how true was her critical perception.

A man who writes a good national ballad discharges the same high service to his country as does the historian, because he embalms, in a form wherein it will always be accessible, an incident which the people desire to preserve. Longfellow proved that he possessed the hammer-like metrical faculty of striking out strong, simple lines wherein incident was everything and the personality of the author nothing. The verses quoted below might well have been written by one of the old balladists, and nothing reveals more clearly the essential strength and simplicity of the poet's nature than the epic swiftness wherewith the action is narrated :

THE WRECK OF THE HESPERUS

It was the schooner Hesperus,
  That sailed the wintry sea ;
And the skipper had taken his little daughtèr,
  To bear him company.

The skipper he stood beside the helm,
  His pipe was in his mouth,
And he watched how the veering flaw did blow
  The smoke now West, now South.

Then up and spake an old Sailôr,
  Had sailed the Spanish Main,
" I pray thee, put into yonder port,
  For I fear a hurricane.

" Last night the moon had a golden ring,
  And to-night no moon we see ! "
The skipper he blew a whiff from his pipe,
  And a scornful laugh laughed he.

Colder and louder blew the wind,
  A gale from the North-east ;
The snow fell hissing in the brine,
  And the billows frothed like yeast.

Down came the storm, and smote amain
  The vessel in its strength ;
She shuddered and paused, like a frighted steed,
  Then leaped her cable's length.

And fast through the midnight dark and drear,
  Through the whistling sleet and snow,
Like a sheeted ghost the vessel swept
  Tow'rds the reef of Norman's Woe.

And ever the fitful gusts between
  A sound came from the land ;
It was the sound of the trampling surf,
  On the rocks and the hard sea-sand.

The breakers were right beneath her bows,
  She drifted a dreary wreck,
And a whooping billow swept the crew
  Like icicles from her deck.

She struck where the white and fleecy waves
  Looked soft as carded wool,
But the cruel rocks they gored her side
  Like the horns of an angry bull.

Her rattling shrouds, all sheathed in ice,
  With the masts went by the board.
Like a vessel of glass she stove and sank.
  Ho ! Ho ! the breakers roared.

At daybreak on the bleak sea-beach
  A fisherman stood aghast,
To see the form of a maiden fair
  Lashed close to a drifting mast.

The salt sea was frozen on her breast,
  The salt tears in her eyes ;
And he saw her hair, like the brown seaweed,
  On the billows fall and rise.

This great poem was reissued in the volume of
1841, with other pieces, under the title " Ballads

and Other Poems.'' Again a marvellous success was achieved. Men felt that in this book they came nearer than ever before to Longfellow the man. There was so much in it that reflected the ordinary everyday life of the poet that his readers seemed to become for the time being his intimate friends and associates. Many of the pieces were so distinctly local in their scenery, position, and atmosphere that they could be identified by residents in the village of Cambridge as forming familiar features in the daily life of the poet-professor.

Not a dweller in Cambridge nor a student of Harvard but would instantly recognize the atmosphere of the poem '' The Village Blacksmith '' as drawn from the '' smithy '' of the brawny local representative of the vocation of Vulcan in Brattle Street. The poet himself had frequently enjoyed a chat with the smith, and the portrait was one of the happiest of those which Longfellow limned in his extensive gallery. Better than any other piece it places on record the poet's admiration for those manly virtues which go to form the sterling heroes of merely commonplace lives. He was, like George Eliot, a firm believer in the innate heroism that lies at the foundation of doing one's duty faithfully and fully amid uninteresting surroundings, and no writer of his century, not even she to whom I have referred as sharing the opinion, has inculcated the truth with more force than Longfellow has done in this poem.

THE VILLAGE BLACKSMITH

Under a spreading chestnut-tree
  The village smithy stands ;
The smith, a mighty man is he,
  With large and sinewy hands ;
And the muscles of his brawny arms
  Are strong as iron bands.

His hair is crisp, and black, and long,
  His face is like the tan ;
His brow is wet with honest sweat,
  He earns whate'er he can,
And looks the whole world in the face,
  For he owes not any man.

Week in, week out, from morn till night,
  You can hear his bellows blow ;
You can hear him swing his heavy sledge,
  With measured beat and slow,
Like a sexton ringing the village bell,
  When the evening sun is low.

And children coming home from school
  Look in at the open door ;
They love to see the flaming forge,
  And hear the bellows roar,
And catch the burning sparks that fly
  Like chaff from a threshing-floor.

He goes on Sunday to the church,
  And sits among his boys ;
He hears the parson pray and preach,
  He hears his daughter's voice,
Singing in the village choir,
  And it makes his heart rejoice.

It sounds to him like her mother's voice,
    Singing in Paradise !
He needs must think of her once more,
    How in the grave she lies ;
And with his hard, rough hand he wipes
    A tear out of his eyes.

Toiling—rejoicing—sorrowing,
    Onward through life he goes ;
Each morning sees some task begin,
    Each evening sees it close ;
Something attempted, something done,
    Has earned a night's repose.

Thanks, thanks to thee, my worthy friend
    For the lesson thou hast taught !
Thus at the flaming forge of life
    Our fortunes must be wrought ;
Thus on its sounding anvil shaped
    Each burning deed and thought.

Another poem in the same volume intimately connected with the poet's life was his piece " To the River Charles." From his study windows in Craigie House he overlooked every day in his life this beautiful stream winding onward, through meadows green as emerald, until lost to sight in the azure of distance. For him this river with its clear crystal tide always had an attraction, as being emblematic of the ideal life of purity and peace. Many a profound lesson its waters had taught him as to how life should be lived to benefit others as well as himself, and, as he says, " this idle song " is his gift in grateful return :

TO THE RIVER CHARLES

River ! that in silence windest
  Through the meadows bright and free,
Till at length thy rest thou findest
  In the bosom of the sea !

Four long years of mingled feeling,
  Half in rest, and half in strife,
I have seen thy waters stealing
  Onward, like the stream of life.

Thou hast taught me, Silent River !
  Many a lesson, deep and long ;
Thou hast been a generous giver,
  I can give thee but a song.

Oft in sadness and in illness,
  I have watched thy current glide,
Till the beauty of its stillness
  Overflowed me, like a tide.

And in better hours and brighter,
  When I saw thy waters gleam,
I have felt my heart beat lighter,
  And leap onward with thy stream.

Not for this alone I love thee,
  Nor because thy waves of blue
From celestial seas above thee
  Take their own celestial hue.

Where yon shadowy woodlands hide thee,
  And thy waters disappear,
Friends I love have dwelt beside thee,
  And have made thy margin dear.

More than this ;—thy name reminds me
  Of three friends, all true and tried ;
And that name, like magic, binds me
  Closer, closer to thy side.

Friends my soul with joy remembers !
  How like quivering flames they start,
When I fan the living embers
  On the hearthstone of my heart !

'Tis for this, thou Silent River !
  That my spirit leans to thee ;
Thou hast been a generous giver,
  Take this idle song from me.

Finally, among the poems in this volume is the one entitled " Maidenhood," which is clearly inspired by his deepening affection for Miss Frances Appleton. To Longfellow she was coming to typify all that was best and noblest in character. He had studied her nature with care, and the deeper he analysed her attributes the more winning and perfect she appeared. Yet in much she was an innocent child, and nothing delighted Longfellow more than to watch the interplay of this subtle union of innocence and worldly wisdom. Warned by the annoyance she had expressed when ardent readers of " Hyperion " persisted in identifying her with Mary Ashburton, Longfellow sang of her as though she were younger than was actually the case.

MAIDENHOOD

Maiden ! with the meek, brown eyes,
In whose orbs a shadow lies,
Like the dusk in evening skies !

LONGFELLOW & HIS POETRY

Thou whose locks outshine the sun,
Golden tresses, wreathed in one,
As the braided streamlets run !

Standing, with reluctant feet,
Where the brook and river meet,
Womanhood and childhood fleet !

O thou child of many prayers !
Life hath quicksands,—Life hath snares !
Care and age come unawares !

Bear a lily in thy hand ;
Gates of brass cannot withstand
One touch of that magic wand.

Bear through sorrow, wrong, and ruth,
In thy heart the dew of youth,
On thy lips the smile of truth.

O, that dew, like balm, shall steal
Into wounds, that cannot heal,
Even as sleep our eyes doth seal ;

And that smile, like sunshine, dart
Into many a sunless heart,
For a smile of God thou art.

Every year, as it passed, revealed new facets
in the wondrously cut jewel of her character,
until he began to realize that if life were to hold
aught of happiness for him in the days that were
to be, those days must be passed in a companion-
ship that would be as subtly sweet as it would be
ideally sympathetic with Frances Appleton.

Such was his mind in the spring of 1842, when,

to the dismay of all his friends and admirers, the report passed from lip to lip that Longfellow was very unwell, and had been ordered away at once to Europe to undergo the " cure " at Marienbad. The truth was he had been working too hard and only needed relaxation. He went to the baths in 1842, spent a pleasant holiday of some months' duration in Germany—the cynosure of all eyes, for already many of his poems had been translated into several of the European languages—then in September of the same year crossed to England, where he was the guest of Charles Dickens, and was hailed with enthusiasm by all the English *literati*. A pleasant visit indeed, because it manifested to him what a large place he had won in the hearts of the English-speaking public. For the first time he realized that he was not merely a popular American verse-writer, but a representative English poet whose works were upon every table, and whose best pieces and lines were graven deep upon every English heart that loved the best in letters.

Longfellow, as he said in his letter to his friend Sumner, was returning to America " with tremendous momentum." Well he might ! Just at his prime alike in years and genius, already one of the most popular poets of the age in both hemispheres, with his horizon unclouded by trouble of any kind, and above all with something more than a vague conviction that the beautiful Frances Appleton was not indifferent to him, little surprise need be felt when we

read in his letters of this date from England :
" Delighted as I am with London, my desire to
be at home again overwhelms every other."

No sooner had he landed and seen his friends
than we find him writing : " Of late my heart
has quite turned my head out of doors." Why
so ? Because he had once more met Frances
Appleton, and absence having made the heart
grow fonder, he realized that he was desperately,
irretrievably in love with the lady of his dreams.
He realized that, great as his success had been,
he had not yet achieved aught that would be
considered commensurate with the genius
bestowed upon him by his God. The meaning
of Frances Appleton's criticisms upon his
" playing with trifles " he now understood in
the light of this new revelation. He doubted
whether he was worthy of her, having failed so
signally to attain the ideal of the poet's office.
The state of his mind at this period may be
judged from the poem " Mezzo Cammin "
(Half-way), which was written at Boppard, on
the Rhine, August 25, 1842, just before leaving
for home. The brilliance of his English welcome
may have laid some of his gloomy apprehensions.
We know, however, that he wrote in an English
album in September 1842 the following sentences
from the penultimate chapter of " Hyperion,"
showing that the frame of mind in which he wrote
" Mezzo Cammin " was only dulled, not dead :

He resolved henceforward not to lean on others, but
to walk self-confident and self-possessed ; no longer
to waste his years in vain regrets, nor await the

57

fulfilment of boundless hopes and indiscreet desires, but to live in the Present wisely, alike forgetful of the Past and careless of what the mysterious Future might bring. And from that moment he was calm and strong.

The lines of the sonnet sound the note of noble purpose too.

MEZZO CAMMIN

Half of my life is gone, and I have let
 The years slip from me and have not fulfilled
 The aspiration of my youth, to build
 Some tower of song with lofty parapet.
Not indolence, nor pleasure, nor the fret
 Of restless passions that would not be stilled,
 But sorrow, and a care that almost killed,
 Kept me from what I may accomplish yet ;
Though, half-way up the hill, I see the Past
 Lying beneath me with its sounds and sights,—
 A city in the twilight dim and vast,
With smoking roofs, soft bells, and gleaming
  lights,—
 And hear above me on the autumnal blast
 The cataract of Death far thundering from
  the heights.

On the voyage across from Britain to America Longfellow fulfilled a long-standing promise. Many of his friends were strongly in favour of the abolition of slavery, and urged the poet to cast the powerful aid of his genius into the scale of the Abolitionists. He was always liable to be touched on the side of his sympathy with physical suffering. He possessed, however, little or none of that intense moral indignation against the iniquity of trafficking in human flesh which inspired the platform philippics of Channing and Lloyd Garrison and the scathing satires and lofty poetic appeals of Whittier and Lowell. His " Poems on Slavery," composed for the most part on the voyage home, are therefore exquisitely musical and loftily pathetic statements of the case from the point of view of one who, although interested in the question, possessed sufficient detachment to take a calm survey, along with the *pros* that were urged in favour of abolition, of the *cons* as well that could be stated against it. The finest piece in the collection is " The Slave's Dream " ; while the one which rouses our indignation most keenly, as revealing to what depths man's inhumanity to man can descend when a planter could actually sell his own daughter to a slaver—

> To be his slave and paramour
> In a strange and distant land—

is " The Quadroon Girl." The heaviest satiric indictment of the whole system, however, is contained in " The Witnesses," which I propose to quote in order to furnish an example of Longfellow as a satirist. He seems too indignant to be sarcastically ironical, he denounces rather than trounces, and in place of discharging such an indictment at the Anti-Abolitionists as would cause them to shrink from the vitriolic intensity of his scorn, he reminds us rather of an angry stump orator who has reached the bottom of his epithet-barrel of

59

vituperation. Had he been more restrained he would have been infinitely more effective. The question inevitably rises to the lips of the reader, "Was the poet absolutely and utterly sincere in his display of indignant contempt, or, *terribile dictu*, did not his thunder savour just a little of the stage?"

THE WITNESSES

In Ocean's wide domains,
  Half buried in the sands,
Lie skeletons in chains,
  With shackled feet and hands.

Beyond the fall of dews,
  Deeper than plummet lies,
Float ships with all their crews,
  No more to sink nor rise.

There the black Slave-ship swims,
  Freighted with human forms,
Whose fettered, fleshless limbs
  Are not the sport of storms.

These are the bones of Slaves ;
  They gleam from the abyss ;
They cry, from yawning waves,
  "We are the Witnesses !"

Within Earth's wide domains
  Are markets for men's lives ;
Their necks are galled with chains,
  Their wrists are cramped with gyves.

Dead bodies, that the kite
  In deserts makes its prey ;
Murders, that with affright
  Scare schoolboys from their play !

All evil thoughts and deeds ;
  Anger, and lust, and pride,
The foulest, rankest weeds
  That choke Life's groaning tide !

These are the woes of Slaves ;
  They glare from the abyss ;
They cry from unknown graves,
  " We are the Witnesses ! "

III

NO sooner had Longfellow returned from Europe than he felt he could no longer delay putting his fortune to the proof by asking Miss Frances Appleton to become his wife. She accepted him, and in July 1843 they were married, to the satisfaction of friends on both sides. An ideal union in every sense of the word it was. The bride, though some ten years the junior of her life-mate, made up for what she lacked in age by the ripe wisdom and sound common sense, united to superb culture and keen intellectual strength, whereof she was possessed. Her beauty was remarkable even in that land of beautiful women, while her ready sympathy and warm affections made her an ideal companion for one whose shyness rendered his manner at first a little chilly until the surface ice of his reticence was thawed. Professor Eric Robertson thus comments on Longfellow's good-fortune :

It was not enough for this earthly-happy poet that he should have had in his youth a helpmate of notice-

61

able beauty and sweetness of character ; in his maturity fortune gave him a nobly planned woman, whose qualities of mind and temper were far above those of most women, rising towards the nature of her husband like flame to flame, while her beauty, if we may judge from written record and the testimony of existing portraits, was truly splendid in its smooth, calm face of a complete oval, set with those "deep, unutterable eyes" of which Longfellow has sung. . . . Mr. Nathan Appleton did not suffer his lovely daughter to pass from him undowered, and bought for the newly married pair the whole of Craigie House and estate to be their home.

The first of Longfellow's productions to be issued after his marriage was " The Spanish Student," a drama of gipsy life, taken from " La Gitanella " of Cervantes. Preciosa, otherwise the Spanish Gipsy, is in reality of noble parentage, having been stolen from her parents in infancy by the gipsies, one of whom, Beltran Cruzado, professes to be her father. By him she has been educated as a dancer, and is betrothed to another gipsy, Bartolomé. She herself, however, loves, and is loved by, Victorian, a student of Alcalá. The latter discovers that a certain *roué*, the Count of Lara, has determined to abduct Preciosa, fights a duel with him for her sake, and defeats him, sparing his life, however, with a sort of contemptuous generosity. The Count thereupon professes friendship fcr Victorian, boasts of favours he has obtained from the dancer, and shows him a ring he declares he has received from her.

Victorian recognizes it, as he thinks, as one
he had given Preciosa, though it is a duplicate
bought on purpose to mislead him. Thereupon
Victorian leaves the girl, believing her to be un-
true. The Count is finally slain by Bartolomé, and
Victorian has his eyes opened to the innocence of
Preciosa, whose real parentage is also discovered.
All ends happily with the pending union of the
lovers, the last scene of all being an attempt on
the part of Bartolomé to shoot Preciosa, only to
be himself shot by Victorian.

We thus briefly describe the plot in order to
indicate two points that deserve attention, first
the striking resemblance that exists between
Victorian, the cultured student-poet of Alcalá,
and Longfellow, the cultured poet-professor of
Harvard. From what he knew of his own
idiosyncrasies the writer had sketched the
character of Victorian. He preferred if possible
to draw from life, and though the drama, *qua*
drama, be worth comparatively little when
critically viewed, the portraits of Preciosa,
Victorian, and Chispa are limned with clearness of outline, individuality of conception, and
wealth of characteristic detail. Longfellow lacked
the true dramatic instinct, his genius being rather
epic than dramatic, and while he could portray
characters excellently, he did so more by
a process of subjective analysis of individual
feelings than by an objective study of the effects
of varying passions and emotions. He had not
the power of developing character by the gradual
evolution of incident like Browning, nor had he

LONGFELLOW & HIS POETRY

Swinburne's lyric passion conjoined with his epic fullness and metrical deftness, moving onward with stately majesty like some brimming river. He resembled Tennyson more, in being an unsurpassed narrator of a story, skilfully laying stress on the salient points and passing over those of minor importance with rapid flight. Longfellow, like many another writer, coveted the glory of excelling in the dramatic arena. Despite the fact that he was recognized as one of the nineteenth century's most popular narrative and lyric poets, his reputation in Clio's domain of epic verse was held by him as of small account, compared with Melpomene's chaplet in tragedy. Notwithstanding its popularity with middle-class readers, notwithstanding the fact that it ranks as by far his best achievement in drama, '' The Spanish Student '' has been regarded by critics as of less value from an artistic point of view than the poorest of his narrative poems. In the latter he grasps and holds the mind of the reader from start to finish ; in drama he seems to lose grip time and again upon the reader's attention, as though the task of maintaining the high level of interest were one of too great difficulty.

The poet's second term of married life extended from 1843 to 1861, and these years were prolific in a notable degree of lofty and noble work. From the day he took her to his heart and home Mrs. Longfellow proved to her husband a helpmate indeed, inasmuch as she ever encouraged him to attempt the highest and best. And after that terrible tragedy of July 10, 1861, had suddenly reft her from his side, when she was literally burned to death before his eyes, her memory remained with him constantly as a stimulus to high achievement ; almost it seemed he strove that her spirit might know its former power upon him was unabated still.

The period in question saw the issue of " The Belfry of Bruges, and other Poems " (1846), a collection of verses written during the preceding three or four years, and including such favourites as " The Old Clock on the Stairs," " The Arsenal at Springfield," " The Arrow and the Song," &c. ; " Evangeline " (1847) ; " Kavanagh " (1849), a prose romance ; " The Seaside and the Fireside " (1850), another collection of miscellaneous poems, but containing that noble national ode, symbolical of the launching of the Republic, " The Building of the Ship " ; " The Golden Legend " (1851) ; " Hiawatha " (1855) ; " Miles Standish " (1858) ; " Tales of a Wayside Inn " (1863). Worthy of note also is the fact that it was subsequent to Mrs. Longfellow's death that her husband so persistently attempted to win laurels in the field of the drama with " New England Tragedies " (1868) ; " The Divine Tragedy " (1871), a dramatic rendering of Christ's life as told in the Gospels ; " Judas Maccabæus " (1872) ; " Masque of Pandora " (1875) ; " Michael Angelo " (posthumous, 1884). In 1872 also the three dramas " The

Divine Tragedy," "The Golden Legend," and "New England Tragedies" were rearranged into a trilogy called "The Christus."

From a careful study of the influence exercised by Mrs. Longfellow over her husband, I am convinced that, had she lived, she would have persuaded him to adhere to the composition of narrative poems, in which department of his art he ranked among the masters, and to relinquish the writing of dramas, for which he had no special talent. How profoundly he relied on her judgment may be estimated from the following anecdote. The poem "The Arsenal at Springfield," contained in the volume "The Belfry of Bruges, and other Poems," was suggested by a speech of Longfellow's friend Charles Sumner on "The True Grandeur of Nations." While walking round the arsenal with Sumner and her husband, Mrs. Longfellow startled them by remarking that the gun-barrels ranged along the walls looked like an organ standing ready for Death to play on it. Longfellow seized on the idea, and reproduced it in the following verse of the poem :

> Ah ! what a sound will rise, how wild and dreary,
>   When the death-angel touches these swift keys !
> What loud lament and dismal Miserere
>   Will mingle with their awful symphonies !

Had she survived we should probably have rejoiced in two or three other studies like those peerless idylls "Evangeline" and "The Courtship of Miles Standish," for which we could well spare such formal and uninspired dramas as "The Divine Tragedy," "Judas Maccabæus," "Michael Angelo," and the "New England Tragedies."

That being so, this seems the proper place to put the question: "What was Longfellow's conception of poetic art and of the function of the poet?"

None knew better than Longfellow himself that though his lips had undoubtedly been touched by the fire of inspiration from the altar of true poetry, he was not one in the apostolic line of succession of the great immortals. His genius was of the eclectic order, ready to seize on, to adopt, and to adapt anything that could in any way contribute to strengthening the impression produced by those imaginative creations that emanated from his soul. To me these verses in his poem on "Oliver Basselin" are suggestive of his own status in the poetic hierarchy, and also convey a clear indication of his conception of the supreme nobility of art:

OLIVER BASSELIN

In the Valley of the Vire
  Still is seen an ancient mill,
With its gables quaint and queer,
  And beneath the window-sill,
    On the stone,
    These words alone:
"Oliver Basselin lived here."

In that darksome mill of stone,
  To the water's dash and din,
Careless, humble, and unknown,
  Sang the poet Basselin
    Songs that fill
    That ancient mill
With a splendour of its own.

Never feeling of unrest
  Broke the pleasant dream he dreamed ;
Only made to be his nest,
  All the lovely valley seemed ;
    No desire
    Of soaring higher
Stirred or fluttered in his breast.

True, his songs were not divine ;
  Were not songs of that high art,
Which, as winds do in the pine,
  Find an answer in each heart ;
    But the mirth
    Of this green earth
Laughed and revelled in his line.

But the poet's memory here
  Of the landscape makes a part ;
Like the river, swift and clear,
  Flows his song through many a heart ;
    Haunting still
    That ancient mill,
In the Valley of the Vire.

The most complete expression of his opinions regarding the poet's office comes to us in the first flight of his " Birds of Passage." There, in " Prometheus ; or, The Poet's Forethought," at

the outset of life, he reveals to us with what high
hopes the poet or teacher begins his career.
Every line seems to sound an autobiographic
note from the depths of his own experience.

PROMETHEUS

OR, THE POET'S FORETHOUGHT

Of Prometheus, how undaunted
    On Olympus' shining bastions
His audacious foot he planted,
Myths are told and songs are chanted,
    Full of promptings and suggestions.

Beautiful is the tradition
    Of that flight through heavenly portals,
The old classic superstition
Of the theft and the transmission
    Of the fire of the Immortals !

First the deed of noble daring,
    Born of heavenward aspiration,
Then the fire with mortals sharing,
Then the vulture,—the despairing
    Cry of pain on crags Caucasian.

All is but a symbol painted
    Of the Poet, Prophet, Seer ;
Only those are crowned and sainted
Who with grief have been acquainted,
    Making nations nobler, freer.

In their feverish exultations,
    In their triumph and their yearning,
In their passionate pulsations,
In their words among the nations,
    The Promethean fire is burning.

Shall it, then, be unavailing,
  All this toil for human culture ?
Through the cloud-rack, dark and trailing,
Must they see above them sailing
  O'er life's barren crags the vulture ?

Such a fate as this was Dante's,
  By defeat and exile maddened ;
Thus were Milton and Cervantes,
Nature's priests and Corybantes,
  By affliction touched and saddened.

But the glories so transcendent
  That around their memories cluster,
And, on all their steps attendant,
Make their darkened lives resplendent
  With such gleams of inward lustre !

All the melodies mysterious,
  Through the dreary darkness chanted ;
Thoughts in attitudes imperious,
Voices soft, and deep, and serious,
  Words that whispered, songs that haunted.

All the soul in rapt suspension,
  All the quivering, palpitating
Chords of life in utmost tension,
With the fervour of invention,
  With the rapture of creating !

Ah, Prometheus ! heaven-scaling !
  In such hours of exultation
Even the faintest heart, unquailing,
Might behold the vulture sailing
  Round the cloudy crags Caucasian !

LONGFELLOW & HIS POETRY

> Though to all there is not given
>   Strength for such sublime endeavour,
> Thus to scale the walls of heaven,
> And to leaven with fiery leaven
>   All the hearts of men for ever ;
>
> Yet all bards, whose hearts unblighted
>   Honour and believe the presage,
> Hold aloft their torches lighted,
> Gleaming through the realms benighted,
>   As they onward bear the message.

So much for the poet's forethought, when the edge of intention was yet unblunted by failure, misunderstanding, and disappointment. Look now at a stanza or two from " Epimetheus ; or, The Poet's Afterthought " :

EPIMETHEUS

OR, THE POET'S AFTERTHOUGHT

> Have I dreamed ? or was it real,
>   What I saw as in a vision,
> When to marches hymeneal
> In the land of the Ideal
>   Moved my thought o'er Fields Elysian ?
>
> What ! are these the guests whose glances
>   Seemed like sunshine gleaming round me ?
> These the wild, bewildering fancies,
> That with dithyrambic dances,
>   As with magic circles, bound me ?
>
> Ah ! how cold are their caresses !
>   Pallid cheeks, and haggard bosoms !
> Spectral gleam their snow-white dresses
> And from loose, dishevelled tresses
>   Fall the hyacinthine blossoms !

O my songs ! whose winsome measures
  Filled my heart with secret rapture !
Children of my golden leisures !
Must ev'n your delights and pleasures
  Fade and perish with the capture ?

Fair they seemed, those songs sonorous
  When they came to me unbidden ;
Voices single, and in chorus,
Like the wild birds singing o'er us
  In the dark of branches hidden.

Disenchantment !   Disillusion !
  Must each noble aspiration
Come at last to this conclusion,
Jarring discord, wild confusion,
  Lassitude, renunciation ?

Him whom thou dost once enamour,
  Thou, belovéd, never leavest ;
In life's discord, strife, and clamour,
Still he feels thy spell of glamour ;
  Him of Hope thou ne'er bereavest.

Weary hearts by thee are lifted,
  Struggling souls by thee are strengthened,
Clouds of fear asunder rifted,
Truth from falsehood cleansed and sifted,
  Lives, like days in summer, lengthened !

Therefore art thou ever dearer,
  O my Sibyl, my deceiver !
For thou mak'st each mystery clearer,
And the unattained seems nearer,
  When thou fill'st my heart with fever !

LONGFELLOW & HIS POETRY

Muse of all the Gifts and Graces !
  Though the fields around us wither,
There are ampler realms and spaces,
Where no foot has left its traces :
  Let us turn and wander thither !

This, of course, raises the question if in Longfellow's case realization quite fulfilled anticipa-
tion as regards his career. He had rated the
office of the poet high ; as life neared evensong did
he bring his mission and his message alike to a
glad and triumphant close ? Let us see. Fully
had he come to know that the poet's niche in the
Temple of Fame was not to be gained without a
severe struggle. In " The Ladder of St. Augustine " he records what was obviously his own
experience in realizing his ideals, artistic and
ethical :

We have not wings, we cannot soar ;
  But we have feet to scale and climb
By slow degrees, by more and more,
  The cloudy summits of our time.

Standing on what too long we bore
  With shoulders bent and downcast eyes,
We may discern, unseen before,
  A path to higher destinies.

Nor deem the irrevocable Past
  As wholly wasted, wholly vain,
If, rising on its wrecks, at last
  To something nobler we attain.

And yet this was the man who, in the imagination of the world, had lived an ideal life of success and happiness. We see here the difference

between the time-ratio of progress as estimated by personal ambition and by the judgment of the public. To the poet fame had been a weary quest, gained only by slow degrees ; to other eyes his seemed a career crowned within an unprecedentedly short time with all the rewards of success.

To Longfellow, however, sorrow, trial, trouble of any kind seemed to be of secondary importance compared with the content that flooded the heart when it was able to feel superior to the world's judgment. He was the victim of a deeply spiritual nature, but he was able to overcome the trouble of the unsatisfied longing of this form of nature with well as to it from the spiritual memory of the natures only unmanly and illogical. Those two beautiful poems " The Bridge " and " The Clock on the Stairs," which are so well known that they do not need quotation, express the longing which Longfellow, in common with thousands of others, felt for a state of happiness that would know no break. Soon he realized, however, that to obtain such a state was something more than had ever fallen to mortal man. Therefore, in these fine lines from " Ultima Thule " we have him on the plane of that lofty faith and hope which he gained :

Vanished now are all the thoughts, the dim, unsatisfied
   longing ;
Sunk are all my dreams aloud into the ocean of dreams ;
While in a harbor of rest my heart is riding at anchor,
Held by the anchor of love, held by the anchors of trust.
74

LONGFELLOW & HIS POETRY

Despite all trials and troubles, to Longfellow it was compensation enough to know that he had brightened darkened lives, strengthened good intentions toward nobler living, and helped to enforce the high standard of duty preached in the " Gospel of Work " as the categorical imperative of life's to-day. Convinced as he was that to every one some talent has been given, he constantly taught that sooner or later an account of the use made of it would be called for. The functions of the poet and the teacher (otherwise the preacher) were to him the same, viz. to better the journey of life, the former seeking to influence men by artistic, the latter by spiritual, methods. Listen to what he says in " Hyperion " (chapter viii.) :

It is better that men should soon make up their minds to be forgotten, and look about them or within them for some higher motive in what they do than the approbation of men, which is Fame—viz. their Duty : that they should be constantly and quietly at work, each in his sphere regardless of effects, and leaving their fame to take care of itself. . . . The resolute, the indomitable will of man can achieve much—at times even this victory over himself, being persuaded that Fame comes only when deserved, and then is as inevitable as destiny, for it is destiny.

In another place in the same chapter he adds under the character of Baron Hohenfels :

Where should the scholar [*i.e.* the poet] live ? In solitude or in society ? In the green stillness of the country where he can hear the heart of Nature beat ; or in the dark, grey town, where he can hear and feel the throbbing heart of man ? I will make answer for him and say in the dark, grey town. O, they do greatly err who think that the stars are all the poetry which cities have, and therefore that the poet's only dwelling should be in sylvan solitudes under the green roof of trees. Beautiful, no doubt, are all the forms of Nature when transfigured by the miraculous power of poetry, hamlets and harvest-fields, and nut-brown waters flowing ever under the forest vast and shadowy, with all the sights and sounds of rural life. But after all what are these but the decorations and painted scenery in the great theatre of human life ? What are they but the coarse materials of the poet's song ? Glorious indeed is the world of God around us, but more glorious the world of God within us. *There* lies the Land of Song : *there* lies the Poet's native land. The River of Life that flows through streets tumultuous, bearing along so many gallant hearts, so many wrecks of humanity ;—the many homes and households, each a little world in itself, revolving round its own fireside, as a central sun ; all forms of human joy and suffering brought into that narrow compass ; and to be in this, and to be a part of this, acting, thinking, rejoicing, sorrowing with his fellow-men—such, such should be the Poet's life. If he would describe the world, he should live in the world.

These were the principles which Longfellow had enunciated early in his literary career, and to which he was faithful even unto the end. To Carlyle he owed much. The " Psalm of Life " embodies the teaching later made famous as the " Gospel of Work " in the sage's " Past and Present." Treatise and poem alike inculcated the supreme necessity of earnestness in life.

LONGFELLOW & HIS POETRY

Both maintained that our duty lies in such a fulfilment of responsible action that each day may find us farther along the upward path of progress. The seer as well as the singer affirmed that though " art is long "—in other words, that what we do is eternal in its effects—the time for achieving our duty is only the brief and fugitive moment called " to-day " or " now." The conclusion, accordingly, which both reached is that if we would be true in every particular to ourselves and to the God who made us, we must act in the present, keeping our hearts clean within, remembering that God overhead sees all, and realizing that if we do not attain success immediately it is our duty to labour on steadily and to wait patiently until we do.

This is the substance of Carlyle's famous " Gospel of Duty " and " Gospel of Work " which he was in those years preaching in England with all the earnestness of a Hebrew prophet. The artistic message given forth by Longfellow to his day and generation was simply this, " What is worth doing at all is worth doing well " ; while the ethico-spiritual dictum inculcated by him in nearly all his poems, and not merely in the " Psalm of Life," is, " Up and doing with a soul for any fate, heart within and God o'erhead." This is just that axiom in his " Gospel of Work," *Laborare est orare,* upon which Carlyle based his epoch-making chapter.

LONGFELLOW & HIS POETRY

In many other poems Longfellow reiterated this doctrine, which he regarded as one of the cardinal principles of a noble life, and upon which he moulded his own. In " The Builders " we have these stanzas :

> Let us do our work as well,
>   Both the unseen and the seen ;
> Make the house, where Gods may dwell
>   Beautiful, entire, and clean.
>
> Else our lives are incomplete,
>   Standing in these walls of Time,
> Broken stairways, where the feet
>   Stumble as they seek to climb.
>
> Build to-day, then, strong and sure,
>   With a firm and ample base ;
> And ascending and secure
>   Shall to-morrow find its place.

Yet another phase of this doctrine on which our poet laid such emphasis in his own life, viz. that of bearing the stress and the strain of the burden of existence that others may be comforted, if not relieved, is to be found in " The Goblet of Life " :

> Let our unceasing, earnest prayer
> Be, too, for light, for strength to bear
> Our portion of the weight of care
> That crushes into dumb despair
>   One half the human race.

Stanzas such as these fell upon feeble and failing hearts like a voice from heaven, instilling new courage into them and stimulating them to fight on, since now they felt that others who had been tried as sorely as themselves sympathized with them.

We have rather run ahead of the principal facts in Longfellow's career in our anxiety to trace the influence of his wife on the development of his genius. We have seen that while she lived she acted the part of the candid but kindly critic, pointing out to her husband wherein his strength and his weakness lay. The former unquestionably centred in narrative poetry, wherein he displayed a genius for picturesque portraiture that fell little short of Chaucer's. Of such poems as " Evangeline," " Hiawatha," " Miles Standish," " Tales of a Wayside Inn," &c., we shall speak presently. Before we do so, however, let us still further adjust the connecting links between the life and the poetry of Longfellow.

In 1849 appeared his prose romance " Kavanagh," another page of autobiography, for under the character of Mr. Churchill he further portrayed himself. The story—if such it could be called—concerned itself with life in the rural parts of Massachusetts about eighty years ago, and consists, as Professor Robertson says, of a series of impressions drawn from the humdrum life of country folk, among whom the only learned and completely discontented person is the village schoolmaster, Mr. Churchill. He felt he had been created to be a poet, and the smallness of his means and leisure and opportunity for the study of life chafed him daily. The moral which the book teaches is one that every writer should lay to heart, viz. the value of " the living present " for the achievement of life's duties. The man who is always " going to do " is the man who does nothing. Mr. Churchill was by nature and temperament a poet, but by vocation a schoolmaster. He was always dreaming of the great romance he was going to write, but of which he never even got the first line begun, because he failed to realize the significance of the old Scots proverb :

> The minutes hained [saved]
> Mean days gained.

On this point Mr. Tirebuck in his introduction to " Longfellow's Prose " says :

We see in the delineation of Mr. Churchill, by nature a poet, by destiny a schoolmaster, indications of Longfellow's early conflicts, his duties battling with his desires, realities with his ideals, his airy fancies with solid facts ; even love, even domesticity occasionally declaring unconscious war against his longings.

All his life Longfellow desired to be free to pursue the vocation of letters unfettered by other ties, yet he felt that duty bade him cling to his professorship. It was the moral warfare between duty and inclination which " Kavanagh " had revealed. Not until 1854, when his books were making him very large returns and when his wife's fortune, settled on her by her father,

80

had so increased in value as to render the poet free from all financial anxieties, did he resign his professorship at Harvard College. His action was dictated by prudence of a type so lofty that it approached moral responsibility, and well would it be if every man of letters would view the matter from the same point of view, for, as Sir Walter Scott said, "Literature is a good crutch, but a bad staff."

The next publication was his collection of poems "Seaside and Fireside," in which we have many personal traits recorded. More than any of his other works this illustrates those attributes of character which made Longfellow what he was, strong, noble, manly, pure, unselfish, and patriotic. The finest poems in the collection are the picturesquely varied "Fire of Drift-wood," the deeply pathetic yet in no wise mawkish "Resignation," and finally that thrillingly patriotic ode which every American whose heart burns with love of fatherland can repeat, "The Building of the Ship."

In this volume he returned a lofty expression of gratitude for the favour wherewith during well-nigh twenty years his works had been received:

If any thought of mine, or sung or told,
  Has ever given delight or consolation,
Ye have repaid me back a thousand fold,
  By every friendly sign and salutation.

Thanks for the sympathies that ye have shown!
  Thanks for each kindly word, each silent token,
That teaches me, when seeming most alone,
  Friends are around us, though no word be spoken.

LONGFELLOW & HIS POETRY

Than these two stanzas of Longfellow there are few indeed that are better known among his works. They appeal intimately and individually to the many varied tastes which find in his poems their satisfying portion alike from an artistic, a literary, and an intellectual point of view. From readers far and near came the gratifying message that in "The Building of the Ship" he had struck a new note, that of "Federal patriotism," which had not been sounded so loud and clear before in the corporate history of the Union. Though within ten years Federal and Confederate were to be at one another's throats in that deadly civil strife through which freedom for the negro was to be secured, no sooner was the noise of battle over than there arose, clear and strong from both sides, the strains of this very Union hymn, which has continued from that day to this the most impressive as it is one of the most popular of all Longfellow's poems. Expressive of his own ardent patriotism as an American Republican, it also revealed the source of that widespread pride which existed among men as varied in descent as could well be the case, viz. that theirs was the land of freedom on whose soil the true tree of liberty grew, bearing as its fruit that universal liberty, equality, and fraternity which were yet to be for the political healing of the nations.

> "Thus," said he, "will we build this ship !
> Lay square the blocks upon the slip,
> And follow well this plan of mine.

LONGFELLOW & HIS POETRY

> Choose the timbers with greatest care ;
> Of all that is unsound beware ;
> For only what is sound and strong
> To this vessel shall belong.
> Cedar of Maine and Georgia pine
> Here together shall combine.
> A goodly frame, and a goodly fame,
> And the 'Union' be her name !
> For the day that gives her to the sea
> Shall give my daughter unto thee ! "

And then the noble pæan at the close :

> Thou, too, sail on, O Ship of State !
> Sail on, O " Union " strong and great !
> Humanity, with all its fears,
> With all the hopes of future years,
> Is hanging breathless on thy fate !
> We know what Master laid thy keel,
> What Workmen wrought thy ribs of steel
> Who made each mast, and sail, and rope,
> What anvils rang, what hammers beat,
> In what a forge and what a heat
> Were shaped the anchors of thy hope !
> Fear not each sudden sound and shock,
> 'Tis of the wave and not the rock ;
> 'Tis but the flapping of the sail,
> And not a rent made by the gale !
> In spite of rock and tempest's roar,
> In spite of false lights on the shore,
> Sail on, nor fear to breast the sea !
> Our hearts, our hopes, are all with thee,
> Our hearts, our hopes, our prayers, our tears,
> Our faith triumphant o'er our fears,
> Are all with thee,—are all with thee !

Longfellow loved the sea with a surpassing

affection, as he abundantly showed in the collection "Seaside and Fireside." He was at home with it in all its moods, finding its placid murmur and its angry roar alike bearing a message to his soul. To him, therefore, the sea was as mighty a teacher as was nature to Wordsworth or man to Browning, and few could interpret its many-languaged speech with more aptness and certainty than he did in such poems as "Seaweed," "The Tide Rises, the Tide Falls," "The Bells of Lynn," "Sir Humphrey Gilbert," "Victor Galbraith," "The Cumberland," &c. In these pieces we actually seem to see the spray whirling high in air and to taste its salt spume on our lips. They literally smack of the ocean. Here are some verses wherein he speaks of the mystery and marvel of the sea :

> . . . His soul was full of longing,
> And he cried with impulse strong,—
> "Helmsman ! for the love of Heaven,
> Teach me, too, that wondrous song ! "

> "Wouldst thou," so the helmsman answered,
> "Learn the secrets of the sea ?
> Only those who brave its dangers
> Comprehend its mystery ! "

> In each sail that skims the horizon,
> In each landward-blowing breeze,
> I behold that stately galley,
> Hear those mournful melodies ;

> Till my soul is full of longing
> For the secret of the sea,
> And the heart of the great ocean
> Sends a thrilling pulse through me.

LONGFELLOW & HIS POETRY

To Longfellow the companion interest to the sea and its wonders was the " fireside," the mystery attaching to home and its influence. This must not be confounded with the " mystery of domesticity," otherwise the conjugal and parental relation, whereof we shall speak in our closing pages. Than the talismanic word " home," the centre of a man's highest and holiest affections, there could be no more powerful "Sesame" to him. The ideas suggested by the word were so varied, and the sympathies aroused were at once of so tender and so catholic a type, that he may be said to have felt with every joy and sorrow that circled round the domestic hearth. To advert to all the poems in which he revealed his love of the fireside would be as impossible as to pass in review all those wherein he showed his passion for the sea. In the poem entitled " The Golden Milestone " he called attention to the infinite vista of possibilities seen from the hearth. By the fireside, he says, old men are seated, seeing ruined cities in the ashes, and asking sadly the restoration of the happiness of the past ; while, on the other hand, by the same centre of attraction are gathered youthful dreamers, building fair " castles in the lowe," and asking the future to give what it cannot. Then he sums up the whole matter in these three notable verses, :

> By the fireside tragedies are acted
> In whose scenes appear two actors only,
> Wife and husband,
> And above them God, the sole spectator.

LONGFELLOW & HIS POETRY

By the fireside there are peace and comfort,
Wives and children, with fair, thoughtful faces,
    Waiting, watching,
For a well-known footstep in the passage.

Each man's chimney is his Golden Milestone,
Is the central point from which he measures
    Every distance
Through the gateways of the world around him.

Another piece in which he paints us an exquisite picture of his warm, fire-illumined library on a wintry night when " the ceaseless rain is falling fast " is " Travels by the Fireside." He declares that the rain

. . . drives me in upon myself
    And to the fireside gleams,
To pleasant books that crowd my shelf,
    And still more pleasant dreams.

I read whatever bards have sung
    Of lands beyond the sea,
And the bright days when I was young
    Come thronging back to me.

Let others traverse sea and land,
    And toil through various climes,
I turn the world round with my hand,
    Reading these poets' rhymes.

Could there be a more delicious picture of the student-poet's sanctum ?

Finally, in that exquisite piece " Resignation,"

how skilfully and powerfully, yet how delicately,
does he refer to his own bereavements and suffer-
ings so as to afford comfort to other fireside
mourners ! Does not the very spirit of all
domestic consolation abide in these stanzas ?

There is no flock, however watched and tended,
　　But one dead lamb is there !
There is no fireside, howsoe'er defended,
　　But has one vacant chair !

The air is full of farewells to the dying,
　　And mournings for the dead ;
The heart of Rachel, for her children crying,
　　Will not be comforted.

Let us be patient ! These severe afflictions
　　Not from the ground arise,
But oftentimes celestial benedictions
　　Assume this dark disguise.

We see but dimly through the mists and vapours ;
　　Amid these earthly damps
What seem to us but sad, funereal tapers
　　May be heaven's distant lamps.

There is no Death ! What seems so is transition ;
　　This life of mortal breath
Is but a suburb of the life elysian,
　　Whose portal we call Death.

She is not dead,—the child of our affection,—
　　But gone unto that school
Where she no longer needs our poor protection,
　　And Christ Himself doth rule.

87

LONGFELLOW & HIS POETRY

In that great cloister's stillness and seclusion,
  By guardian angels led,
Safe from temptation, safe from sin's pollution,
  She lives, whom we call dead.

Day after day we think what she is doing
  In those bright realms of air˙;
Year after year, her tender steps pursuing,
  Behold her grown more fair.

Thus do we walk with her, and keep unbroken
  The bond which nature gives,
Thinking that our remembrance, though unspoken,
  May reach her where she lives.

Not as a child shall we again behold her ;
  For when with raptures wild
In our embraces we again enfold her,
  She will not be a child ;

But a fair maiden, in her Father's mansion,
  Clothed with celestial grace ;
And beautiful with all the soul's expansion
  Shall we behold her face.

And though at times impetuous with emotion
  And anguish long suppressed,
The swelling heart heaves moaning like the ocean,
  That cannot be at rest,—

We will be patient, and assuage the feeling
  We may not wholly stay ;
By silence sanctifying, not concealing,
  The grief that must have way.

LONGFELLOW & HIS POETRY

IV

LONGFELLOW'S essential greatness was expressed in the short occasional poem, whereof he unquestionably takes rank as one of the world's masters, rather than in those longer narrative works which he mistakenly supposed to be his greatest achievements. Of the latter, however, he produced two or three epics in miniature which are as perfect as anything of the kind could be. The fact must, however, be admitted that while in these he found a notable outlet for his thick-coming fancies, there is in them a marked aloofness from life, nature, and from his own special surroundings. That may be occasioned by the choice of themes, those of his smaller poems being very frequently taken from incidents happening in either his own experience or those of his friends, while the subjects of his longer poems, "Evangeline," "The Courtship of Miles Standish," "Hiawatha," "Tales of a Wayside Inn," and "Keramos," to say nothing of his dramas, are drawn from scenes that lay either distant from his own time and land or were descriptive of a race alien to his own.

For this reason, then, we find fewer allusions to his own life and doings in the latter than the former. Yet his longer poems are by no means wholly destitute of such references.

"Evangeline" is a tale of the deportation from Nova Scotia in 1755 of the Acadian or

French farmers—not, be it noted, by order of the British Government, but at the instance of a self-constituted tribunal consisting of the Governor of Nova Scotia, the Chief Justice of the province, and two British admirals. One of the most cruel wrongs ever perpetrated by an irresponsible junta on a set of innocent and unsuspecting people, it is a stain on the memory of King George II that he allowed it to go unpunished.

The plot of the story is simple, being merely the separation of the heroine, an Acadian maiden named Evangeline, from her lover Gabriel, her search for him during many long years, and how at last she found him in a hospital, dying. The unaffected pathos of the poem, the exquisite vignettes of scenery, the lifelike and sharply differentiated characters, with the warm glow of imagination playing upon the poem from start to finish, all conduce to render it one of the most delightful narrative pieces in American literature. The metrical form the poet chose was one of great difficulty, being no other than that English hexameter which a master of metre like Swinburne declared to be a "bastard measure," and of which Matthew Arnold said that it *might* be possible to carry literary artifice so far as to put together English hexameters capable of scansion by long and short syllables. Clough, Hawtrey, Charles Kingsley, Howells, and Bayard Taylor have all essayed the so-called impossible measure with success. Undoubtedly, however, the best answer to Swinburne's strictures is—

to read " Evangeline " ! A delightful poem
in hexametric verse had actually been composed and had installed itself as one of the
popular favourites of English-speaking peoples
when the critics were saying such a thing was
impossible. Longfellow certainly wrote hexameters in English as no other poet has ever
succeeded in doing. Even Tennyson, marvellous
as was his mastery over most other forms of
metre, if more correct, was more stiff in his
handling of this measure. He has not the easy
grace of Longfellow's line, simply because he
seemed afraid to vary the cæsural pause with the
same freedom. Clough in the " Bothie of Tober-
na-Vuolich," and Kingsley in " Andromeda,"
come nearer the American's high standard,
but they were so tied by the conventions of
Oxford scholarship that they frequently per-
mitted classicism to override common sense.

In Longfellow's case, moreover, the theme lent
itself to this style of treatment. There were no
violent emotions to be portrayed, no strong situations to be worked up. The narrative had simply
to flow onward through placid reaches of description until the last sad scene of recognition
would be attained, when the natural end would
come.

The success which attended " Evangeline "
was so great that when a theme illustrative of
the early Puritan life in America was suggested
to the poet he reverted to the English hexameters
which had stood him in such good stead before.
Although a period of eleven years separated the

respective dates of their composition, and although "Hiawatha," properly speaking, should be considered between them, it will tend to brevity of treatment if we examine them together.

"The Courtship of Miles Standish" is concerned with the wooing by Miles Standish, the Captain of Plymouth, of a beautiful Puritan maiden named Priscilla, who had come out in the "Mayflower" with him. Though brave as a lion himself, Standish dreads the refusal of his suit, and therefore employs as his go-between John Alden, "his friend and household companion." John Alden, who, by the way, was also a "Mayflower" voyager and a distant ancestor of the poet, did not relish his task, for, truth to tell, he too loved the maiden, and had just been writing home

Letters . . . full of the name of Priscilla,
Full of the name and the fame of the Puritan maiden,
    Priscilla.

John Alden goes and pleads his friend's cause, but does not make much headway until Priscilla begins to criticize the Captain. Here it is that Longfellow shows his marvellous knowledge of the human heart. Alden had stammered and hesitated in his avowal of Standish's love, but with Priscilla's criticism comes the determination loyally to defend his friend, even although it chances to be the woman whom he himself loves that utters the words of blame, until,

. . . as he warmed and glowed, in his simple and
    eloquent language,
Quite forgetful of self, and full of the praise of his rival,

Archly the maiden smiled, and, with eyes overrunning
    with laughter,
Said, in a tremulous voice, " Why don't you speak for
    yourself, John ? "

Alden rushes from the house, amazed and
bewildered. On relating the scene to the Captain
the latter overwhelms him with reproaches, and
goes off to drive back the Indians who are
threatening the infant settlement. Alden feels
he could not marry Priscilla while Standish
lives, but while he is eating his heart out
with sorrow news is brought that the brave
Captain has been killed in battle with the
Indians. Nothing now seems to stand in the
way of the union of the lovers, and they are
married, when suddenly, as the ceremony con-
cludes, a grim and warlike figure stands before
them. It is the Captain returned victorious,
eager also to beg forgiveness for his hasty words,
and anxious to be the first to congratulate the
bride and bridegroom.

I summarize the plot of " Miles Standish "
because I wish to point out the increase in
wisdom which the experience of years brought
to Longfellow. When we compare " Miles
Standish " with " Evangeline " we note at
once greater insight into the artistic evolution
of theme, a firmer grip upon the gradual development of the action, so that nothing irrelevant or
of merely secondary moment shall find place
therein to divert attention from the main issues ;
a profounder knowledge of the mysteries of

character-drawing and how a telling portrait is to be best achieved by the aid of incident and not by mere analysis ; finally, a subtler perception of the complexities of character. Formerly, in "Evangeline," the poet's personages were typical of a single virtue : now they are representative of many traits, some of them absolutely antagonistic to one another; for instance, the Captain of Plymouth, who is so good yet so choleric, and John Alden, who is so gentle yet so proud.

What then is the secret of that epic art which makes both of these works so telling ? Their simplicity and directness ! They go straight to the heart of the theme, like Homer, and then, with all Homer's swiftness, tell the story without any irrelevancies. That is where Longfellow excels Tennyson. He is truly an unsurpassed *raconteur*. The art of metrical narrative he had studied keenly and closely. Had he written the "Idylls of the King" we should not have had to deplore the introduction of so many matters that are not in the very slightest degree germane to the spirit of the story.

But there is a further reason. In both poems Longfellow was describing scenes out of his own life and experience. A far-travelled man amid European lands and peoples, he had also gone widely throughout the length and breadth of America. From Canada to Florida, from Nova Scotia to San Francisco, he had journeyed at various seasons of his life, so that he seldom, if ever, described a scene that he had not visited. He was always anxious about local colour in his poems, and before writing those matchless descriptions of the Mississippi and its tributary waters he went and saw the country. Hurried though his visit was, it gave him what he needed. Here is the description which has so often been praised as an almost photographic picture of Louisiana river scenes—that scene which brings Evangeline and Gabriel so near one another that their boats pass, but, like ships that pass in the night, unwitting of each other's proximity :

Thus ere another noon they emerged from those shades ; and before them
Lay, in the golden sun, the lakes of the Atchafalaya.
Water-lilies in myriads rocked on the slight undulations
Made by the passing oars, and, resplendent in beauty, the lotus
Lifted her golden crown above the heads of the boatmen.
Faint was the air with the odorous breath of magnolia blossoms,
And with the heat of noon ; and numberless sylvan islands,
Fragrant and thickly embowered with blossoming hedges of roses,
Near to whose shores they glided along, invited to slumber.
Soon by the fairest of these their weary oars were suspended.
Under the boughs of Wachita willows, that grew by the margin,
Safely their boat was moored ; and scattered about on the greensward,

Tired with their midnight toil, the weary travellers
    slumbered.
Over them vast and high extended the cope of a cedar.
Swinging from its great arms, the trumpet-flower and
    the grape-vine
Hung their ladder of ropes aloft like the ladder of
    Jacob,
On whose pendulous stairs the angels ascending,
    descending,
Were the swift humming-birds that flitted from
    blossom to blossom.
Such was the vision Evangeline saw as she slumbered
    beneath it.
Filled was her heart with love, and the dawn of an
    opening heaven
Lighted her soul in sleep with the glory of regions
    celestial.

  Nearer and ever nearer, among the numberless
    islands,
Darted a light, swift boat, that sped away o'er the water,
Urged on its course by the sinewy arms of hunters
    and trappers.
Northward its prow was turned, to the land of the
    bison and beaver.
At the helm sat a youth, with countenance thoughtful
    and careworn.
Dark and neglected locks overshadowed his brow,
    and a sadness
Somewhat beyond his years on his face was legibly
    written.
Gabriel was it, who, weary with waiting, unhappy
    and restless,
Sought in the Western wilds oblivion of self and of
    sorrow.

Swiftly they glided along, close under the lee of the
island,

But by the opposite bank, and behind a screen of
palmettos,

So that they saw not the boat, where it lay concealed
in the willows,

And undisturbed by the dash of their oars, and unseen,
were the sleepers.

Angel of God was there none to awaken the slumbering
maiden.

Swiftly they glided away, like the shade of a cloud on
the prairie.

After the sound of their oars on the tholes had died
in the distance,

As from a magic trance the sleepers awoke, and the
maiden

Said with a sigh to the friendly priest,—" O Father
Felician !

Something says in my heart that near me Gabriel
wanders."

That is noble descriptive writing, but it bears
the stamp of a peculiar diffuseness which might
almost be described as youthful, though the poet
was thirty-seven when he penned it. Note, however, the difference when ten years later he wrote
" Miles Standish." How condensed are the
descriptions ! Yet every picture is adequate.
Does the advantage of increasing years explain
all the mystery ? Nay, verily ! There is another
factor to be taken into account. To the scenes
described in the following passage he did not
merely pay a hasty visit and then, having noted
the details, hurry away. Among scenes akin to
those of the latter poem he had lived all his life,

and was so familiar with their salient features
that the non-essential ones were forgotten.
There is all the difference in the world between
impressions conveyed by a single visit and
impressions that are stamped by the intercourse of years. Compare this picture with the
foregoing :

So the strong will prevailed, and Alden went on his
errand,
Out of the street of the village, and into the paths of
the forest,
Into the tranquil woods, where blue-birds and robins
were building
Towns in the populous trees, with hanging gardens of
verdure,
Peaceful, aërial cities of joy and affection and freedom.
All around him was calm, but within him commotion
and conflict,
Love contending with friendship, and self with each
generous impulse.
To and fro in his breast his thoughts were heaving
and dashing,
As in a foundering ship, with every roll of the vessel,
Washes the bitter sea, the merciless surge of the ocean !
" Must I relinquish it all ? " he cried, with a wild
lamentation,
" Must I relinquish it all, the joy, the hope, the illu-
sion ?
Was it for this I have loved, and waited, and wor
shipped in silence ?
Was it for this I have followed the flying feet and the
shadow
Over the wintry sea, to the desolate shores of New
England ! "

Or this other :

Many a mile had they marched, when at length the village of Plymouth
Woke from its sleep, and arose, intent on its manifold labours.
Sweet was the air and soft ; and slowly the smoke from the chimneys
Rose over roofs of thatch, and pointed steadily eastward ;
Men came forth from the doors, and paused and talked of the weather,
Said that the wind had changed, and was blowing fair for the May Flower ;
Talked of their Captain's departure, and all the dangers that menaced,
He being gone, the town, and what should be done in his absence.
Merrily sang the birds, and the tender voices of women
Consecrated with hymns the common cares of the household.
Out of the sea rose the sun, and the billows rejoiced at his coming ;
Beautiful were his feet on the purple tops of the mountains ;
Beautiful on the sails of the May Flower riding at anchor,
Battered and blackened and worn by all the storms of the winter.
Loosely against her masts was hanging and flapping her canvas,
Rent by so many gales, and patched by the hands of the sailors.
Suddenly from her side, as the sun rose over the ocean,

Darted a puff smoke and floa... seaward ; anon
   rang
Loud over field ... ... the cannon's ..., and the
   echoes
Heard and repeated the ... ... the signal-gun o...
   dep... ...

I think ... ... w... ... ... wi... ...
... ...
m... ... ... an... ...
No... ... that all. I... ... ...
Stand... ." ...e have a personal element ... ... is
almost .... 'ine.' ...ohn
Al...n ... many traits tha... ...fellow
witt... ... or unwittingly drew from ... ...wn
nat... . The " ...dreamy elegant sch...r h...
th... graces of s...h and skill in ... ...urning
p...ses " was s... an apt d...tion of t...
...t himself. Nor ... histo... John Alden
... ...epos wholly without pa...el in that of t...
... himself. Hawthorne pointed this out, a...
L...ng'ellow ... ...fe, with
wor...s " M...y our ... ... happ... s
that ... ny ancestor John Alden and the P... n
maid ... ...riscilla." Unconscious reprod... ... of
...s ow... ...its is always more or l... ...able
with ... ..."

We now ... to consider " Hiawa...a,... and
to note whether ... poet has impressed ... ... any
of his ...wn ...tributes, ...intus... ...r of ... wn
traits into ...e characters. ... ...e
only attempt worthy of '... ... ...
" re... ... amidst hi... ...tive surro...ings.

That it was successful is evidenced by its continued popularity. Although suggested to the poet as regards both measure and treatment by the Finnish epic " Kalevala," it is absolutely original in all other respects. Hiawatha is a semi-divine personage, like Buddha in Hindu mythology and Prometheus in Grecian, who came to earth to benefit certain races and to teach them the arts of peace. He seems to have had several incarnations, like Buddha, for, while called Hiawatha among the Ojibways on the southern shores of Lake Superior, where the locale of the poem is laid, he is also known as Manabozho, Michabou, Chiabo, and Tarenyawagon among other tribes to whom he likewise appeared. Even as Scott put the narrative of " The Lay of the Last Minstrel " into the mouth of the last of the minstrels, who related it to the widowed duchess of the ill-fated Monmouth, so Longfellow professed to have received the scenes in the life of Hiawatha

> From the lips of Nawadaha,
> The musician, the sweet singer.

The poet veils his identity so completely in this metrical chronicle of Indian life, customs, and traditions that only once does he speak directly under his own character. That is in the " Introduction," when the occasion warranted the dropping of the veil. He desired to proclaim that " Hiawatha " was a nature-poem, one in which, like Wordsworth, he was to seek to portray the shy, shrinking divinity of the mighty

American " forests primeval." Accordingly,
taking the reader by the hand, as it were, he
says :

> Ye who love the haunts of Nature,
> Love the sunshine of the meadow,
> Love the shadow of the forest,
> Love the wind among the branches,
> And the rain-shower and the snow-storm,
> And the rushing of great rivers
> Through their palisades of pine-trees,
> And the thunder in the mountains,
> Whose innumerable echoes
> Flap like eagles in their eyries ;—
> Listen to these wild traditions,
> To this Song of Hiawatha !
>
> Ye who love a nation's legends,
> Love the ballads of a people,
> That like voices from afar off
> Call to us to pause and listen,
> Speak in tones so plain and childlike,
> Scarcely can the ear distinguish
> Whether they are sung or spoken ;—
> Listen to this Indian legend,
> To this Song of Hiawatha !
>
> Ye whose hearts are fresh and simple
> Who have faith in God and Nature,
> Who believe, that in all ages
> Every human heart is human,
> That in even savage bosoms
> There are longings, yearnings, strivings,
> For the good they comprehend not,
> That the feeble hands and helpless,
> Groping blindly in the darkness,
> Touch God's right hand in that darkness,
> And are lifted up and strengthened :—

> Listen to this simple story,
> To this Song of Hiawatha !
>   Ye, who sometimes, in your rambles
> Through the green lanes of the country,
> Where the tangled barberry-bushes
> Hang their tufts of crimson berries
> Over stone walls grey with mosses,
> Pause by some neglected graveyard,
> For a while to muse, and ponder
> On a half-effaced inscription,
> Written with little skill of song-craft,
> Homely phrases, but each letter
> Full of hope, and yet of heart-break,
> Full of all the tender pathos
> Of the Here and the Hereafter ; —
> Stay and read this rude inscription !
> Read this Song of Hiawatha !

Could any confession of faith be more simple, more direct, yet more tellingly true than that presented in the above extract ? Within the scope of these fifty lines we learn more of Longfellow's ardent nature-worship than from the whole body of his other verse—learn to appreciate those deep and holy lessons he received amid nature's rural haunts, from the sunshine of the meadow, from the shadow of the forest, from the wind amid the branches, from the rain-shower and the snow-storm, from the rushing of great rivers through their palisades of pine-trees, from the thunder amid the mountains with its innumerable echoes.

Further, in the passage quoted above we see his fondness for the ballad literature of the nation in preference to any other phase of its literary expression. Is it not true that the ballads of a people sound like the mystic voices of its inner life, oftentimes revealing racial traits that are absolutely unsuspected ? From the ballads of a race we learn its early aspirations, its patriotism, and the ideals which it has set before it in the shaping of its existence.

Nor is that all the revelation of Longfellow's inner soul which reaches us. He was not ashamed to nail the colours of his creed to the moral masthead, and to proclaim the fact that the secrets and subtle teachings of nature led him steadily and surely up to nature's God. He not only saw written across every created unit, " The Hand that made us is divine," but he came to realize that even in the most degraded of human hearts there are implanted certain ethical first principles which lead the ignorant savage to long, to yearn, and to strive for the good he can only dimly comprehend, groping ever blindly toward the light, until he touches God's hand amid the darkness and is thereafter led upward and onward toward the morning star of faith, which points ever more and more to the dawning of the perfect day.

Again, with what exquisite tenderness and feeling he touches on the pathos which underlies the record of obscure yet duty-devoted lives, whose sole memorial is some half-effaced inscription in a lonely and neglected graveyard ! Yet these had their days of hope and joy and expectation, doing their duty faithfully in the sight of God and man, though now they lie in far-distant and forgotten graves. He treats of the same theme as Gray in his immortal " Elegy," the conclusion reached by both being the same : Fulfil the demands of duty's call, and leave the rest to God. This doctrine of the paramount claim of duty is also shadowed forth by Mudjekeewis after the terrible conflict between him and his son Hiawatha :

> " Hold, my son, my Hiawatha !
> 'Tis impossible to kill me,
> For you cannot kill the immortal.
> I have put you to this trial,
> But to know and prove your courage ;
> Now receive the prize of valour !
> " Go back to your home and people,
> Live among them, toil among them,
> Cleanse the earth from all that harms it,
> Clear the fishing-grounds and rivers,
> Slay all monsters and magicians,
> All the Wendigoes, the giants,
> All the serpents, the Kenabeeks,
> As I slew the Mishe-Mokwa,
> Slew the Great Bear of the mountains.
> " And at last when Death draws near you,
> When the awful eyes of Pauguk
> Glare upon you in the darkness,
> I will share my kingdom with you,
> Ruler shall you be thenceforward
> Of the Northwest-Wind, Keewaydin,
> Of the home-wind, the Keewaydin."

Did Longfellow infuse aught of his own characteristic qualities into any of the personages

of the narrative ? By many of his contem-
poraries the view was maintained that unwittingly the poet had portrayed himself under
the guise of Chibiabos, the musician. Certainly
when he lay dead amid the mourning of the
entire world many of the obituary notices
referred to him as Chibiabos, and as he was
carried to his grave his requiem was chanted in
words taken from his own poem :

> He is dead, the sweet musician !
> He the sweetest of all singers !
> He has gone from us forever,
> He has moved a little nearer
> To the Master of all music,
> To the Master of all singing !
> O my brother, Chibiabos !

Here is the passage in which Chibiabos is
described, so that readers may judge for themselves of its applicability to the poet :

> Two good friends had Hiawatha,
> Singled out from all the others,
> Bound to him in closest union,
> And to whom he gave the right hand
> Of his heart, in joy and sorrow ;
> Chibiabos, the musician,
> And the very strong man, Kwasind.
>   Straight between them ran the pathway,
> Never grew the grass upon it ;
> Singing-birds, that utter falsehoods,
> Story-tellers, mischief-makers,
> Found no eager ear to listen,
> Could not breed ill-will between them,
> For they kept each other's counsel,

Spake with naked hearts together,
Pondering much, and much contriving
How the tribes of men might prosper.

Most beloved by Hiawatha
Was the gentle Chibiabos,
He the best of all musicians,
He the sweetest of all singers.
Beautiful and childlike was he,
Brave as man is, soft as woman,
Pliant as a wand of willow,
Stately as a deer with antlers.

When he sang, the village listened ;
All the warriors gathered round him,
All the women came to hear him ;
Now he stirred their souls to passion,
Now he melted them to pity.

From the hollow reeds he fashioned
Flutes so musical and mellow,
That the brook, the Sebowisha,
Ceased to murmur in the woodland,
That the wood-birds ceased from singing
And the squirrel, Adjidaumo,
Ceased his chatter in the oak-tree,
And the rabbit, the Wabasso,
Sat upright to look and listen.

Yes, the brook, the Sebowisha,
Pausing, said, " O Chibiabos,
Teach my waves to flow in music,
Softly as your words in singing ! "

Yes, the blue-bird, the Owaissa,
Envious, said, " O Chibiabos,
Teach me tones as wild and wayward,
Teach me songs as full of frenzy ! "

Yes, the Opechee, the robin,
Joyous said, " O Chibiabos,

Teach me tones as sweet and tender,
Teach me songs as full of gladness ! ''
    And the whippoorwill, Wawonaissa,
Sobbing, said, '' O Chibiabos,
Teach me tones as melancholy,
Teach me songs as full of sadness ! ''
    All the many sounds of nature
Borrowed sweetness from his singing,
All the hearts of men were softened
By the pathos of his music ;
For he sang of peace and freedom,
Sang of beauty, love, and longing ;
Sang of death, and life undying
In the Islands of the Blessed,
In the kingdom of Ponemah,
In the land of the Hereafter
    Very dear to Hiawatha
Was the gentle Chibiabos,
He the best of all musicians,
He the sweetest of all singers ;
For his gentleness he loved him,
And the magic of his singing.

The last of Longfellow's narrative poems was that delightful collection brought together from well-nigh all the literatures of the world, and entitled '' Tales of a Wayside Inn.'' Issued in 1863, the work was largely undertaken by Longfellow to drown, in intense intellectual labour, the sorrow that threatened to overwhelm him after his second wife's terrible death. Having been reading Chaucer's '' Canterbury Tales '' once more, with an interest as profound as ever, the idea was suggested to his mind that something on similar lines might be attempted in the New World. The difficulty was to secure a sufficient posse of well-contrasted yet interesting characters to act as the storytellers. Accordingly we have a Landlord (who is in addition a landed proprietor and a Justice of the Peace), a Student profoundly versed in chivalry, a Spanish Jew from Alicante, a Theologian, a Norse Musician, a Sicilian, and a Poet. These individuals were all drawn from life. " In the town of Sudbury, twenty miles from Cambridge," says Professor E. S. Robertson, "was an old inn called ' The Red Horse Tavern,' a large, irregular, low-roofed hostelry surrounded by fine trees. Here lived as landlord and squire of the parish, with a coat of arms, a gentleman of good descent, called Howe. To Howe's bar-parlour Longfellow brought in imagination T. W. Parsons, the translator of Dante (the Poet) ; Luigi Monti, a Sicilian ; Professor Treadwell, of Harvard Theological Faculty (the Theologian) ; Henry Ware Wales, the well-known scholar (the Student) ; the violinist, Ole Bull (the Musician) ; and a notable Jew called Israel Edulei (the Spanish Jew)."

In the "Prelude," which for vigour and clearness of portraiture falls little short of the work of Chaucer himself, we have these men deftly delineated. The one with whom Longfellow would feel himself most in affinity would be the Poet, and the character is drawn with a loving tenderness that glorified the subject. We saw what Longfellow's conception of the

poet's function was ; let us now see how he
limns the Poet in life :

> A Poet, too, was there, whose verse
> Was tender, musical, and terse ;
> The inspiration, the delight,
> The gleam, the glory, the swift flight,
> Of thoughts so sudden, that they seem
> The revelations of a dream,
> All these were his ; but with them came
> No envy of another's fame ;
> He did not find his sleep less sweet
> For music in some neighbouring street,
> Nor rustling hear in every breeze
> The laurels of Miltiades.
> Honour and blessings on his head
> While living, good report when dead,
> Who, not too eager for renown,
> Accepts, but does not clutch, the crown.

During one of the " Interludes " he interposes
some remarks on a matter which those who
have studied their Longfellow carefully know
was one that our poet had very much at heart,
the suppression of cruelty to animals—cruelty
oftentimes quite unwittingly committed, yet
gathering to itself none the less surely its guilt
and shame. The story of " The Bell of Atri "
had won applause, when the Poet burst forth
with these arguments unmistakably characteristic of Longfellow :

> " Yes, well your story pleads the cause
> Of those dumb mouths that have no speech,
> Only a cry from each to each
> In its own kind, with its own laws ;

Something that is beyond the reach
Of human power to learn or teach,—
An inarticulate moan of pain
Like the immeasurable main
Breaking upon an unknown beach."

Thus spake the Poet with a sigh ;
Then added, with impassioned cry,
As one who feels the words he speaks,
The colour flushing in his cheeks,
The fervour burning in his eye :
" Among the noblest in the land,
Though he may count himself the least,
That man I honour and revere
Who without favour, without fear,
In the great city dares to stand
The friend of every friendless beast,
And tames with his unflinching hand
The brutes that wear our form and face,
The were-wolves of the human race ! "
Then paused, and waited with a frown,
Like some old champion of romance,
Who, having thrown his gauntlet down,
Expectant leans upon his lance ;
But neither Knight nor Squire is found
To raise the gauntlet from the ground,
And try with him the battle's chance.

Then, in the " Poet's Tale " entitled " The
Birds of Killingworth " there comes in the same
connexion the following lofty appeal for the
preservation of song-birds :

" The thrush that carols at the dawn of day
    From the green steeples of the piny wood ;
The oriole in the elm ; the noisy jay,
    Jargoning like a foreigner at his food ;

LONGFELLOW & HIS POETRY

The blue-bird balanced on some topmost spray,
　Flooding with melody the neighbourhood ;
Linnet and meadow-lark, and all the throng
That dwell in nests and have the gift of song.

" You slay them all ! and wherefore ? for the gain
　Of a scant handful more or less of wheat,
Or rye, or barley, or some other grain,
　Scratched up at random by industrious feet,
Searching for worm or weevil after rain !
　Or a few cherries, that are not so sweet
As are the songs these uninvited guests
Sing at their feast with comfortable breasts.

" Do you ne'er think what wondrous beings these ?
　Do you ne'er think who made them, and who taught
The dialect they speak, where melodies
　Alone are the interpreters of thought ?
Whose household words are songs in many keys,
　Sweeter than instrument of man e'er caught !
Whose habitations in the tree-tops even
Are half-way houses on the road to heaven !

" Think, every morning when the sun peeps through
　The dim, leaf-latticed windows of the grove,
How jubilant the happy birds renew
　Their old melodious madrigals of love !
And when you think of this, remember too
　'Tis always morning somewhere, and above
The awakening continents, from shore to shore,
Somewhere the birds are singing evermore.

" Think of your woods and orchards without birds !
　Of empty nests that cling to boughs and beams !
As in an idiot's brain remembered words
　Hang empty 'mid the cobwebs of his dreams !

Will bleat of flocks or bellowing of herds
　　Make up for the lost music, when your teams
Drag home the stingy harvest, and no more
The feathered gleaners follow to your door ?

" What ! would you rather see the incessant stir
　　Of insects in the windrows of the hay,
And hear the locust and the grasshopper
　　Their melancholy hurdy-gurdies play ?
Is this more pleasant to you than the whirr
　　Of meadow-lark, and her sweet roundelay,
Or twitter of little field-fares, as you take
Your nooning in the shade of bush and brake ?

" You call them thieves and pillagers ; but know
　　They are the wingèd wardens of your farms,
Who from the corn-fields drive the insidious foe,
　　And from your harvests keep a hundred harms ;
Even the blackest of them all, the crow,
　　Renders good service as your man-at-arms,
Crushing the beetle in his coat of mail,
And crying havoc on the slug and snail.

" How can I teach your children gentleness,
　　And mercy to the weak, and reverence
For Life, which, in its weakness or excess,
　　Is still a gleam of God's omnipotence,
Or Death, which, seeming darkness, is no less
　　The selfsame light, although averted hence,
When by your laws, your actions, and your speech,
You contradict the very things I teach ? "

V

DEEPLY is it to be regretted that Longfellow forsook the domain of the narrative poem for that of the drama. The requisite qualifications for the making of strong dramatic situations out of materials by no means promising were not his. At all times he needed a large canvas whereon to work. Not having this in the drama, his plays are rather charming specimens of dialogue than dramas in the proper sense of the word.

The subjects of his plays were largely alien to Transatlantic life and customs, and but few references occur either to the circumstances of the poet's own existence or to his ideas on art and thought, with the reciprocal influence they exercise on each other.

"The Spanish Student," to which we have already referred, though more of a dramatic poem than a drama, has a peculiar reference to his speculations on life, death, and futurity, on the " Hereafter " as seen from the " Here," and on " Long Ago " as regarded from the " Now." There is scarcely a poem of Longfellow's without a reference to the Kantian-Fichtean metaphysic popularized by Carlyle, and such a passage as this speech by Victorian, the Student of Alcalá,

> . . . Our feelings and our thoughts
> Tend ever on, and rest not in the Present.
> As drops of rain fall into some dark well,

> And from below comes a scarce audible sound,
> So fall our thoughts into the dark Hereafter,
> And their mysterious echo reaches us,

shows how deeply steeped was his soul in the mysticism which was so prevalent at that time. Longfellow, I repeat, was so profoundly affected by the philosophy that scarcely a poem was written by him at this epoch that did not contain some allusion to the " Now " and the " Then," the " Ever " and the " Never," the " Here " and the " Hereafter." Witness " The Old Clock on the Stairs," " The Bridge," " The Occultation of Orion," " A Gleam of Sunshine," and many others that could be named among his " occasional " verse. In his dramas, also, it is this distinctive feature that compensates for their lack of personal traits and links them on to the life of the poet.

" The Golden Legend " has achieved great popularity, almost entirely owing to the beauty of the character of Elsie. Prince Henry of Vautsberg, the hero, is a mouthing, sentimental, mawkish fool. He has contracted a strange disease which cannot be cured

> . . . unless
> Some maiden of her own accord
> Offers her life for that of her lord,
> And is willing to die in his stead.

He wanders away in search of health, is imposed upon by Lucifer, and induced to take a medicine, " Catholicon," which gives the

Devil some sort of power over him. At last he
reaches a cottage in the Odenwald, where he is
hospitably entertained by the owner and his
wife, both of the peasant class. The eldest
daughter of the house falls in love with the
Prince, and, hopeless of ever marrying him,
resolves to die for him. He actually accepts
the sacrifice. Elsie and he proceed to Salerno,
where the sacrifice is to take place. But there
Henry is miraculously cured, marries Elsie,
and all ends happily. As E. C. Stedman says,
the piece is a brilliant conglomerate. Though
Longfellow owed not a little to Goethe's
"Faust," the originality of much of the play is
beyond question, while certain of the characters
are ably drawn and not without strokes of
shrewd humour. There is only one passage in
" The Golden Legend " that seems to recall the
poet and his personality, and that is the *padrone's*
description of a sea-scene during the voyage
of Prince Henry and Elsie to Salerno. In it
appears all Longfellow's intense love of the
sea, every phase being lovingly dwelt upon,
with the behaviour of the vessel under the
influence of waves and wind :

> *Il Padrone.* The wind upon our quarter lies,
> And on before the freshening gale,
> That fills the snow-white lateen sail,
> Swiftly our light felucca flies.
> Around, the billows burst and foam ;
> They lift her o'er the sunken rock,
> They beat her sides with many a shock,
> And then upon their flowing dome

They poise her, like a weathercock !
Between us and the western skies
The hills of Corsica arise ;
Eastward, in yonder long blue line,
The summits of the Apennine,
And southward, and still far away,
Salerno, on its sunny bay.
You cannot see it, where it lies. . . .
I must entreat you, friends, below !
The angry storm begins to blow,
For the weather changes with the moon.
All this morning, until noon,
We had baffling winds, and sudden flaws
Struck the sea with their cat's-paws.
Only a little hour ago
I was whistling to Saint Antonio
For a capful of wind to fill our sail,
And instead of a breeze he has sent a gale.
Last night I saw Saint Elmo's stars,
With their glimmering lanterns, all at play
On the tops of the masts and the tips of the
    spars. . . .
Ha ! that is the first dash of the rain,
With a sprinkle of spray above the rails,
Just enough to moisten our sails,
And make them ready for the strain.
See how she leaps, as the blasts o'ertake her,
And speeds away with a bone in her mouth !
Now keep her head toward the south,
And there is no danger of bank or breaker.
With the breeze behind us, on we go ;
Not too much, good Saint Antonio !

We search in vain throughout those lifeless
later dramas, the " New England Tragedies," the " Judas Maccabæus," " The Divine

Tragedy," "The Masque of Pandora," and
"Michael Angelo," for a single revelation of
the poet's own personal characteristics. In none
of the *dramatis personæ* do we find evidence
that the poet has reproduced in them aught of
his own traits or qualities. As he grew older
a sort of separation or aloofness from his
work appears in all he wrote. That intimate
infusion of his own personality into his poems
visible in his earlier occasional pieces—nay,
in most of these even to the very end—is
well-nigh totally absent from his later dramas
after "The Golden Legend." Infinitesimal
though the degree is in which the personal
element enters into his dramatic work at all,
after the publication of "The Golden Legend"
this quality virtually appears no more. After
his wife's death, followed quickly by those of
his father and mother, of Professors Felton
and Ware, of Charles Sumner, and of Agassiz,
his intense interest in life seemed to die down.
Like Horace he lived for the day, and his attach-
ment was rather to men and things of the past
than to those of the present. His dramas of this
period, therefore, are for the most part melancholy reading, owing to that atmosphere of
profound sadness and gloom in which they are
steeped. Only in the prologues to the "New
England Tragedies"—rather, too, in the first
prologue than in the second—and in the dedication of his posthumously published tragedy of
"Michael Angelo" do we find any indication
of a personal element entering into what he

wrote. Here is the prologue to the first of the
" New England Tragedies." It gives a vivid
picture of that primitive New England life
which still lingered on into his own early years.

To-night we strive to read, as we may best,
This city, like an ancient palimpsest ;
And bring to light, upon the blotted page,
The mournful record of an earlier age,
That, pale and half effaced, lies hidden away
Beneath the fresher writing of to-day.

Rise, then; O buried city that hast been ;
Rise up, rebuilded in the painted scene,
And let our curious eyes behold once more
The pointed gable and the penthouse door,
The Meeting-house with leaden-latticed panes,
The narrow thoroughfares, the crooked lanes !

Rise, too, ye shapes and shadows of the Past,
Rise from your long-forgotten graves at last ;
Let us behold your faces, let us hear
The words ye uttered in those days of fear !
Revisit your familiar haunts again—
The scenes of triumph and the scenes of pain,
And leave the footprints of your bleeding feet
Once more upon the pavement of the street !

Nor let the Historian blame the Poet here,
If he perchance misdate the day or year
And group events together, by his art,
That in the Chronicles lie far apart ;
For as the double stars, though sundered far,
Seem to the naked eye a single star,
So facts of history, at a distance seen,
Into one common point of light convene.

 " Why touch upon such themes ? " perhaps some
     friend
May ask, incredulous ; " and to what good end ?

LONGFELLOW & HIS POETRY

Why drag again into the light of day
The errors of an age long passed away ? "
I answer : " For the lesson that they teach :
The tolerance of opinion and of speech.
Hope, Faith, and Charity remain,—these three ;
And greatest of them all is Charity."
   Let us remember, if these words be true,
That unto all men Charity is due ;
Give what we ask ; and pity, while we blame,
Lest we become co-partners in the shame,—
Lest we condemn, and yet ourselves partake,
And persecute the dead for conscience' sake.
   Therefore it is the author seeks and strives
To represent the dead as in their lives,
And lets at times his characters unfold
Their thoughts in their own language, strong
    and bold ;
He only asks of you to do the like :
To hear him first, and, if you will, then strike.

Longfellow's noble ethical code, writ large over his whole life, is put on record here : " Do unto others as ye would they should do unto you," the maxim he professed and practised throughout his long life of seventy-five years.

Here, too, is the dedication of the " Michael Angelo," which sounds that earnestly hopeful note for the final good of all things which formed so conspicuous an article in his creed. Albeit his own outlook upon life was sad during his latest years, it was by no means cheerless. True, Sorrow's crown of Sorrow is remembering happier things, and it was so in his case ; but amid all these bitter-sweet memories of the days that were dead his spiritual eyesight could look beyond the present to the glory of the coming dawn, when all things shall be changed and we shall know even as we are known. That is the note which is struck in the dedication :

> Nothing that is shall perish utterly,
> But perish only to revive again
> In other forms, as clouds restore in rain
> The exhalations of the land and sea.
> Men build their houses from the masonry
> Of ruined tombs ; the passion and the pain
> Of hearts, that long have ceased to beat, remain
> To throb in hearts that are, or are to be.
> So from old chronicles, where sleep in dust
> Names that once filled the world with trumpet
> tones,
> I build this verse ; and flowers of song have
> thrust
> Their roots among the loose, disjointed stones,
> Which to this end I fashion as I must.
> Quickened are they that touch the Prophet's
> bones.

Longfellow was a matchless translator from many languages, and the felicity as well as facility wherewith he was able to reproduce the ideas of one language in the words of another is nothing short of marvellous. His glorious rendering of Dante's " Divina Commedia " still holds rank among the best. Published during the years 1867 to 1870, it has never waned in popularity with scholars and the general public alike, and that which it has held so long it is not likely now to lose.

LONGFELLOW & HIS POETRY

VI

MANY critics have been puzzled to account
for the notable accession of imaginative and artistic power visible in Longfellow's occasional poems during the last twelve
years of his life. After a careful examination
of the matter from many points of view I have
come to the conclusion that this result was due
to the prolonged and intensely minute study of
the precise shades of meaning possessed by
words of closely analogous import necessitated
by his translation of Dante. Previous to 1867
his language, as the vesture of thought, was
decidedly loose-girt in the special forms of
speech employed. In other words, the expression
of the thought was not tightly braced up to
the exact shade of meaning indicated. After
his exacting labours entailed by the translation of the " Divina Commedia " the alliance
between thought and its expression became
in his case so intimate that little divergence,
comparatively speaking, can be detected between
them.

During the closing decade of his life he seems
to have relinquished largely the composition
of works that demanded a large canvas. His
essays in the drama were over save for his
posthumous play, " Michael Angelo." He
devoted himself now to the preparation of works
brief and occasional in character, and his
success was commensurate with the enormous

pains he expended upon them. Of these there are several poems in " Ultima Thule," Parts I and II, to which I desire to call attention, because they throw a very illuminating light on the poet's ways of life and thought during the years when age was creeping upon him.

That profound and widely cultured critic Professor George Saintsbury has said in his introduction to the selections from Longfellow in the " Golden Poets Series," regarding these occasional poems :

And so we are left with those shorter poems which, if people would only throw away mistaken traditional theories of poetry, are the real test of a poet's gift, unless he is an altogether exceptional person as well as poet, like Dante. . . . All Longfellow's best work is of this kind, and there is a great deal of it. He never lost his skill at it, from the early " Voices of the Night " to the singularly beautiful introduction of " Ultima Thule."

I am entirely of Professor Saintsbury's opinion. We could spare a great deal of Longfellow's longer narrative verse for a few more such poems as " Chrysaor," " The Secret of the Sea," " King Witlaf's Drinking Horn," " The Ladder of St. Augustine," " Haunted Houses," " My Lost Youth," " The Golden Milestone," " Santa Filomena," " Sandalphon," and those which cast light upon his personal opinions and characteristics. To a few of the latter I desire to call more particular attention. One of the virtues for which we prize Longfellow as a

123

poet is his absolute lack of self-conceit, that smug satisfaction with self that never misses an opportunity, metaphorically speaking, of patting its own vanity on the back. Great as had been his success in literature, Longfellow nevertheless felt that he had not completely realized his own ideals. In that beautiful poem "Loss and Gain," written during the final decade of his life, he subjects his own literary achievements to the keenest and most unsparing analysis, the verdict being far from in his own favour :

> When I compare
> What I have lost with what I have gained,
> What I have missed with what attained,
>   Little room do I find for pride.
>
> I am aware
> How many days have been idly spent ;
> How like an arrow the good intent
>   Has fallen short or been turned aside.
>
> But who shall dare
> To measure loss and gain in this wise ?
> Defeat may be victory in disguise ;
>   The lowest ebb is the turn of the tide.

Longfellow's artistic and ethical ideals were so high that what to many another man would have been a perfectly legitimate course to adopt, in his eyes was absolutely barred. If he were not a consummate literary artist like Tennyson, it was not because his ideal of duty as regards excellence of work was a whit lower than that of the author of the " Idylls of the King." In a sonnet entitled " Possibilities " he again insists upon work being done with every faculty strained to the utmost. For him to be a " slacker "—if an expression savouring of slang may be pardoned—or to fail wittingly in putting forth his best effort on every occasion was as impossible as for Emerson to have wilfully deceived. Here is his artistic creed expressed in the sonnet aforesaid :

> Where are the Poets, unto whom belong
> The Olympian heights ; whose singing shafts
>   were sent
> Straight to the mark, and not from bows half
>   bent,
> But with the utmost tension of the thong ?
> Where are the stately argosies of song,
> Whose rushing keels made music as they went
> Sailing in search of some new continent,
> With all sail set, and steady winds and strong ?
> Perhaps there lives some dreamy boy, untaught
> In schools, some graduate of the field or street,
> Who shall become a master of the art,
> An admiral sailing the high seas of thought,
> Fearless and first, and steering with his fleet
> For lands not yet laid down in any chart.

Longfellow, therefore, early recognized the glory attaching to noble work nobly done, and to his last hour of life he insisted on the unfailing applicability of the trite old maxim, " What is worth doing at all is worth doing well." The secret of his high ideals lay in the fact already stated, that he maintained the poet to be merely

the channel of his message, which came to him
from the " vast Unknown " as thought inspired
by the Author of Existence. The poet's duty is
so to deliver the message he receives—that is to
say, so to envelop it in artistic and telling form—
that it may have an effect commensurate with the
greatness of the Sender. Longfellow enunciates
this doctrine of the " Divine Inspirer of Song "—
an idea at least cognate in content to Wordsworth's " Divine Spirit in Nature "—in a poem
of rare spiritual elevation and beauty of metrical
form, entitled " The Poet and his Songs,"
written only some eighteen months before his
death.

THE POET AND HIS SONGS

As the birds come in the spring,
　We know not from where ;
As the stars come at evening
　From the depths of the air ;

As the rain comes from the cloud,
　And the brook from the ground ;
As suddenly, low or loud,
　Out of silence a sound.

As the grape comes to the vine,
　The fruit to the tree ;
As the wind comes to the pine,
　And the tide to the sea ;

As come the white sails of ships
　O'er the ocean's verge ;
As comes the smile to the lips ;
　The foam to the surge ;

> So come to the Poet his songs,
>   All hitherward blown
> From the misty land, that belongs
>   To the vast Unknown.
>
> His, and not his, are the lays
>   He sings ;—and their fame
> Is his, and not his ;—and the praise
>   And the pride of a name.
>
> For voices pursue him by day,
>   And haunt him by night,
> And he listens, and needs must obey,
>   When the angel says, "Write ! "

The same idea is somewhat differently voiced in "The Abbot Joachim." The poet's creed here was more ethical than spiritual, in that his desire was to impress upon men that the highest worship is expressed in the noblest work. The essence of worship is service ; therefore he who rises to nobler heights of self-sacrifice or to a round of deeds of more beneficence justifies the rationale of his existence in infinitely higher measure than he who virtually besieges heaven with prayer, bombarding it with petitions in which the interests of self predominate. "Watch and pray," but the watching is the first and prime duty :

> Then reigned the Son ; His covenant
> Was peace on earth, good-will to man :
> With Him the reign of Law began.
> He was the Wisdom and the Word,
> And sent His angels ministrant,
> Unterrified and undeterred,

> To rescue souls forlorn and lost,
> The troubled, tempted, tempest-tost,
> To heal, to comfort, and to teach. . . .
> These Ages now are of the past ;
> And the Third Age begins at last.
> The coming of the Holy Ghost,
> The reign of Grace, the reign of Love
> Brightens the mountain-tops above,
> And the dark outline of the coast. . . .
> My work is finished !   I am strong
> In faith and hope and charity :
> For I have written the things I see,
> The things that have been and shall be,
> Conscious of right, nor fearing wrong ;
> Because I am in love with Love,
> And the sole thing I hate is Hate ;
> For Hate is death ; and Love is life,
> A peace, a splendour from above ;
> And Hate, a never-ending strife,
> A smoke, a blackness from the abyss
> Where unclean serpents coil and hiss !
> Love is the Holy Ghost within ;
> Hate, the unpardonable sin !
> Who preaches otherwise than this
> Betrayeth his Master with a kiss !

A similar idea is expressed in the " Interlude " following " The Saga of King Olaf," and there Longfellow once more sounds that note of faith in which he was to live and die—the creed of the poet of which we come now to speak :

> " Ah ! to how many Faith has been
> No evidence of things unseen,
> But a dim shadow, that recasts
> The creed of the Phantasiasts

For whom no Man of Sorrows died,
For whom the Tragedy Divine
Was but a symbol and a sign,
And Christ a phantom crucified !

" For others a diviner creed
Is living in the life they lead.
The passing of their beautiful feet
Blesses the pavement of the street,
And all their looks and words repeat
Old Fuller's saying, wise and sweet,
Not as a vulture, but a dove,
The Holy Ghost came from above."

That being the opinion Longfellow entertained of the almost sacred mission of poetry alike in its substance and its form, what was his belief regarding that which lay behind both these parts of poetry—to wit, the ethico-spiritual faith which attunes life to " the perfect music of a psalm " ? Longfellow was a sincerely religious man, albeit he revealed little of his own spiritual communings to the world at large. To him " the Life Here " and " the Life Hereafter " were as the obverse and the reverse of the same medal. Both were probationary periods of service, the one being complementary to the other, so that the friendships and the loves of earth, sublimated and sanctified, would be continued behind the veil. This is very beautifully expressed in the poem " Auf Wiedersehen," written in memory of his lifelong friend, the publisher James T. Fields. The poet's intimate circle had been sadly broken in these last years.

I

AUF WIEDERSEHEN

Until we meet again !   That is the meaning
Of the familiar words that men repeat
    At parting in the street.
Ay, yes, till then ! but when death intervening
Rends us asunder, with what ceaseless pain
    We wait for the Again !

The friends who leave us do not feel the sorrow
Of parting as we feel it who must stay
    Lamenting day by day,
And knowing, when we wake upon the morrow,
We shall not find in its accustomed place
    The one belovèd face.

It were a double grief if the departed,
Being released from earth, should still retain
    A sense of earthly pain ;
It were a double grief if the true-hearted
Who loved us here, should on the farther shore
    Remember us no more.

Believing, in the midst of our afflictions,
That death is a beginning, not an end,
    We cry to them, and send
Farewells, that better might be called predictions,
Being foreshadows of the future thrown
    Into the vast Unknown.

Faith overleaps the confines of our reason,
And if by faith, as in old times was said,
    Women received their dead
Raised up to life, then only for a season
Our partings are, nor shall we wait in vain
    Until we meet again.

A deeper note, however, is struck in that wonderful poem written only a few weeks before his death, in which he anticipates the meeting with her who had been to him the better part of life itself, and with his daughter Fanny, who had died young. The ties of life had one by one been broken, and now the aged poet seems waiting solitary and lonely, yet eagerly hopeful, for the wished-for call, "Come up hither." Perfect love, as he said, had cast out all fear, seeing that his faith was like that of the little child : "Lo, my Father doeth all things well!"

VIA SOLITARIA

Alone I walk the peopled city,
    Where each seems happy with his own ;
Oh ! friends, I ask not for your pity—
    I walk alone.

No more for me yon lake rejoices,
    Though moved by loving airs of June ;
Oh ! birds, your sweet and piping voices
    Are out of tune.

In vain for me the elm tree arches
    Its plumes in many a feathery spray ;
In vain the evening's starry marches
    And sunlit day.

In vain your beauty, Summer flowers ;
    Ye cannot greet these cordial eyes ;
They gaze on other fields than ours—
    On other skies.

The gold is rifled from the coffer,
  The blade is stolen from the sheath ;
Life has but one more boon to offer,
    And that is—Death.

Yet well I know the voice of Duty,
  And, therefore, life and health must crave,
Though she who gave the world its beauty
    Is in her grave.

I live, O lost one ! for the living
  Who drew their earliest life from thee,
And wait, until with glad thanksgiving
    I shall be free.

For life to me is as a station
  Wherein apart a traveller stands—
One absent long from home and nation,
    In other lands.

And I, as he who stands and listens,
  Amid the twilight's chill and gloom,
To hear, approaching in the distance,
    The train for home.

For death shall bring another mating
  Beyond the shadows of the tomb,
On yonder shores a bride is waiting
    Until I come.

In yonder field are children playing,
  And there—oh ! vision of delight !—
I see the child and mother straying
    In robes of white.

Thou, then, the longing heart that breakest,
  Stealing the treasures one by one,
I'll call Thee blessèd when Thou makest
    The parted—one.

LONGFELLOW & HIS POETRY

The last poem which Longfellow wrote, "The Bells of San Blas," was instinct with the triumphant faith that gleamed forth clear and bright from all his work. Written only a day or two before his death, it appeared in print after he had gone to his rest, and was accepted by his many readers with love and reverence as the dying words of him who had given them of his best so long. As a great American critic says: "The concluding lines seemed to foretell the speedy coming of a new Social Evangel when men would understand each other better and class wars would come to an end." Whether or no, he whose words they were had nobly done his share to promote the common brotherhood of mankind. Of those who on that snowy March day in 1882 stood around his open grave in the cemetery of Mount Auburn, near Cambridge, amid the vast concourse of mourners which assembled from all quarters to render to his dust the last tribute of respect, not one but must have realized that the world was desperately the poorer by the loss of this great and gracious spirit, whose desire in all his works had been to bind men closer together and to lift them nearer to God.

THE BELLS OF SAN BLAS

What say the Bells of San Blas
To the ships that southward pass
     From the harbour of Mazalan ?
To them it is nothing more
Than the sound of surf on the shore—
     Nothing more to master or man.

133

But to me, a dreamer of dreams,
To whom what is and what seems
   Are often one and the same,—
The Bells of San Blas to me
Have a strange, wild melody,
   And are something more than a name.

For bells are the voice of the Church ;
They have tones that touch and search
   The hearts of young and old ;
One sound to all, yet each
Lends a meaning to their speech,
   And the meaning is manifold.

They are a voice of the Past,
Of an age that is fading fast,
   Of a power austere and grand,
When the flag of Spain unfurled
Its folds o'er this Western world,
   And the Priest was lord of the land.

The chapel that once looked down
On the little seaport town
   Has crumbled into dust ;
And on oaken beams below
The bells swing to and fro,
   And are green with mould and rust.

" Is, then, the old faith dead,"
They say, " and in its stead
   Is some new faith proclaimed,
That we are forced to remain
Naked to sun and rain,
   Unsheltered and ashamed ?

" Once, in our tower aloof,
We rang over wall and roof
    Our warnings and our complaints ;
And round about us there,
The white doves filled the air
    Like the white souls of the saints.

" The saints !   Ah, have they grown
Forgetful of their own ?
    Are they asleep or dead,
That open to the sky
Their ruined Missions lie,
    No longer tenanted ?

" Oh, bring us back once more
The vanished days of yore,
    When the world with faith was filled ;
Bring back the fervid zeal,
The hearts of fire and steel,
    The hands that believe and build.

" Then from our tower again
We will send over land and main
    Our voices of command,
Like exiled kings who return
To their thrones, and the people learn
    That the Priest is lord of the land ! "

O Bells of San Blas, in vain
Ye call back the Past again !
    The Past is deaf to your prayer :
Out of the shadows of night
The world rolls into light ;
    It is daybreak everywhere.

VII

LONGFELLOW, as I have already said, has frequently been styled "the poet of domesticity and childhood." Time and again in lines of surpassing beauty he has celebrated the abiding joy of the domestic relation and how it both sublimates and sanctifies the character and the emotions. While he never rose to so lofty a note of conjugal affection as that struck by Coventry Patmore in "The Angel in the House," he has uttered in such pieces as "Footsteps of Angels," "It is not always May," "Mezzo Cammin," "Twilight," "The Fire of Drift-wood," "Hiawatha," "Haunted Houses," "Stay, stay at home, my heart, and rest," "From my Armchair," "Elegiac," to mention only a few of the poems in which a domestic chord has been sounded, strains in praise of family life and the love of home as deeply sincere as they are profoundly pathetic.

Longfellow in both his marriages had been so ideally happy that little wonder need be felt that he straightway constituted himself the warm panegyrist of the conjugal relation. To the full he had drained its cup of pure and varied pleasure, and only just and fitting it was that he should declare with no uncertain sound his testimony on the matter. Nor has he failed to do so effectively. In the first of the two poems I have chosen for citation the poet is looking from a stormy evening into the comfortable pleasures of a cosy library. With the sense of labour well and honestly discharged he steps as it were out of the gloom into the domestic gladness.

THE DAY IS DONE

The day is done, and the darkness
 Falls from the wings of Night,
As a feather is wafted downward
 From an eagle in his flight.

I see the lights of the village
 Gleam through the rain and the mist,
And a feeling of sadness comes o'er me,
 That my soul cannot resist :

A feeling of sadness and longing
 That is not akin to pain,
And resembles sorrow only
 As the mist resembles the rain.

Come, read to me some poem,
 Some simple and heartfelt lay,
That shall soothe this restless feeling,
 And banish the thoughts of day.

Not from the grand old masters,
 Not from the bards sublime,
Whose distant footsteps echo
 Through the corridors of Time.

For, like strains of martial music,
 Their mighty thoughts suggest
Life's endless toil and endeavour ;
 And to-night I long for rest.

Read from some humbler poet,
  Whose songs gushed from his heart,
As showers from the clouds of summer,
  Or tears from the eyelids start ;

Who, through long days of labour,
  And nights devoid of ease,
Still heard in his soul the music
  Of wonderful melodies.

Such songs have power to quiet
  The restless pulse of care,
And come like the benediction
  That follows after prayer.

Then read from the treasured volume
  The poem of thy choice,
And lend to the rhyme of the poet
  The beauty of thy voice.

And the night shall be filled with music,
  And the cares that infest the day
Shall fold their tents, like the Arabs,
  And as silently steal away.

In the second of the poems he is sitting in the library looking out into the glory that is upon the face of nature. He lets his eye rest in turn upon the peaceful benediction which the silver moon is pouring upon the crowded roofs of the town and then upon the silent sea and the autumn wood. He watches the lights around him, each one being in turn extinguished, then turns with a sigh to his own cheery lamp within. The picture is one of great beauty, being drawn with splendid restraint, yet vivid realism :

MUSINGS

I sat by my window one night,
  And watched how the stars grew high ;
And the earth and skies were a splendid sight
  To a sober and musing eye.

From heaven the silver moon shone down
  With gentle and mellow ray,
And beneath the crowded roofs of the town
  In broad light and shadow lay.

A glory was on the silent sea,
  And mainland and island too,
Till a haze came over the lowland lea,
  And shrouded that beautiful blue.

Bright in the moon the autumn wood
  Its crimson scarf unrolled,
And the trees like a splendid army stood
  In a panoply of gold !

I saw them waving their banners high,
  As their crests to the night wind bowed,
And a distant sound on the air went by,
  Like the whispering of a crowd.

Then I watched from my window how fast
  The lights all around me fled,
As the wearied man to his slumber passed,
  And the sick one to his bed.

All faded save one, that burned
  With distant and steady light ;
But that, too, went out,—and I turned
  Where my own lamp within shone bright !

139

Thus, thought I, our joys must die,
 Yes—the brightest from earth we win :
Till each turns away, with a sigh,
 To the lamp that burns brightly within.

Than Longfellow no one has celebrated with greater charm and pathos the joys and the sorrows of childhood. With ready sympathy he enters into the feelings, the aspirations, the longings, the hopes, and the fears of boyhood and maidenhood. We have, in truth, had profounder analysts of the child-heart, like Stevenson, or Christina Rossetti, or William Blake, but we have never had a singer who so thoroughly exemplified the affirmative side of the axiom, "Not to sympathize is not to understand." Longfellow sympathizes so keenly with all that interests children because he understands their nature and feelings so well.

Only such a man could have written those poems, "To a Child," "My Lost Youth," "Children," "Weariness," to mention only one or two out of many. Perhaps the finest of all his child-poems are " The Open Window " and " The Children's Hour," the former of which produces its effect by the feeling of the absence of the loved ones, the latter by the sense of their presence.

THE OPEN WINDOW

The old house by the lindens
 Stood silent in the shade,
And on the gravelled pathway
 The light and shadow played.

I saw the nursery windows
　　Wide open to the air ;
But the faces of the children,
　　They were no longer there.

The large Newfoundland house-dog
　　Was standing by the door ;
He looked for his little playmates,
　　Who would return no more.

They walked not under the lindens,
　　They played not in the hall !
But shadow, and silence, and sadness
　　Were hanging over all.

The birds sang in the branches,
　　With sweet, familiar tone ;
But the voices of the children
　　Will be heard in dreams alone !

And the boy that walked beside me,
　　He could not understand
Why closer in mine, ah ! closer,
　　I pressed his warm, soft hand !

THE CHILDREN'S HOUR

Between the dark and the daylight,
　　When the night is beginning to lower,
Comes a pause in the day's occupations,
　　That is known as the Children's Hour.

I hear in the chamber above me
　　The patter of little feet,
The sound of a door that is opened,
　　And voices soft and sweet.

LONGFELLOW & HIS POETRY

From my study I see in the lamplight,
  Descending the broad hall stair,
Grave Alice, and laughing Allegra,
  And Edith with golden hair.

A whisper, and then a silence :
  Yet I know by their merry eyes
They are plotting and planning together
  To take me by surprise.

A sudden rush from the stairway,
  A sudden raid from the hall !
By three doors left unguarded
  They enter my castle wall !

They climb up into my turret
  O'er the arms and back of my chair ;
If I try to escape they surround me :
  They seem to be everywhere.

They almost devour me with kisses,
  Their arms about me entwine,
Till I think of the Bishop of Bingen
  In his Mouse-Tower on the Rhine !

Do you think, O blue-eyed banditti,
  Because you have scaled the wall,
Such an old moustache as I am
  Is not a match for you all !

I have you fast in my fortress,
  And will not let you depart,
But put you down into the dungeon
  In the round-tower of my heart.

And there will I keep you for ever,
  Yes, for ever and a day,
Till the walls shall crumble to ruin
  And moulder in dust away !

LONGFELLOW & HIS POETRY

Such then, briefly, is Longfellow, viewed in the relationship which exists between his life and his poetry. Space only remains to answer the question : Has the poet in any of his works revealed the secret hidden in his verse of that marvellously subtle charm wherewith he speaks with equal force and equal witchery to young and old alike ? Yes ! He is the student of nature as well as of art, and of art as well as of nature. Accordingly the key to the mystery appears in these lines from " Kéramos " wherewith I close this volume :

> Art is the child of Nature ; yes,
> Her darling child, in whom we trace
> The features of the mother's face,
> Her aspect and her attitude ;
> All her majestic loveliness
> Chastened and softened and subdued
> Into a more attractive grace,
> And with a human sense imbued.
> He is the greatest artist, then,
> Whether of pencil or of pen,
> Who follows Nature.   Never man,
> As artist or as artisan,
> Pursuing his own fantasies,
> Can touch the human heart, or please,
> Or satisfy our nobler needs,
> As he who sets his willing feet
> In Nature's footprints light and fleet,
> And follows fearless where she leads.

BIBLIOGRAPHY

For the further study of Longfellow the following may be recommended :

Riverside Edition of Longfellow's Works, with " Life " by Samuel Longfellow.

Robertson, Prof. E. S. : " Life " in " Great Writers Series."

Higginson, T. W. : " Life "—" American Men of Letters."

Saintsbury, Prof. G. : Introduction to " Selected Works " in " The Golden Poets."

Stedman, E. C. : " American Poets," the chapter on Longfellow.

Howells, W. D. : " Literary Friends and Acquaintance," chapter on Longfellow.

Stebbing, William : " Five Centuries of English Verse," article in vol. ii. on Longfellow's art and influence.

Trent, W. P. : " American Literature."

DATE OF ISSUE OF THE WORKS OF LONGFELLOW

Outre-Mer, 1830 ; Hyperion, 1839 ; Voices of the Night, 1839 ; Ballads and other Poems, 1841 ; The Spanish Student, 1843 ; Poems on Slavery, 1844 ; Evangeline, 1847 ; Kavanagh, 1849 ; The Seaside and the Fireside, 1849 ; The Golden Legend, 1851 ; Hiawatha, 1855 ; The Courtship of Miles Standish, 1858 ; Tales of a Wayside Inn, 1863-74 ; Translation of Dante, 1865-67 ; The Divine Tragedy, Parts I and II, 1871 ; New England Tragedies, 1868-71 ; The Masque of Pandora, 1874 ; Judas Maccabæus, 1876 ; Michael Angelo, 1882.